Rainbows
in
Puddles

by

Mary "Corky" Treacy Thompson

BLUE MUSTANG
P R E S S

Blue Mustang Press
Boston, Massachusetts

First printing

Back cover drawing by Peggy Egan

Back cover author's photo by:
Laura Mahony Photography, Denver Colorado

ISBN: 978-1-935199-19-9
PUBLISHED BY BLUE MUSTANG PRESS
www.bluemustangpress.com
Boston, Massachusetts

Printed in the United States of America

Gratefully dedicated to
L. Dale Lund, PhD
and
Rev. Charles Berdahl, DMin

Also by Mary "Corky" Treacy Thompson

Moving Van Christmas

Hammond's Candies:
History Handmade in Denver

Contents

List of Illustrations
Prologue
Acknowledgments
Chronology
Family and Associates of Ed and Duane Vikman
Introduction 15
Chapter One - The Last Christmas 19
Chapter Two - Sons No More 25
Chapter Three - Unwanted 29
Chapter Four - Underground Life 35
Chapter Five - Outside Faces 43
Chapter Six - The Executioner 55
Chapter Seven - Heartbreak 61
Chapter Eight - School Daze 65
Chapter Nine - Waffles for Breakfast 69
Chapter Ten - Carlsons' Farm: The Early Years 75
Chapter Eleven - Carlsons' Farm: Boys Working Men's Jobs 87
Chapter Twelve - Carlsons' Farm: Fruits of Our Labor 93
Chapter Thirteen - Carlsons' Farm: Deliverance 99
Chapter Fourteen - Life Looks Up 105
Chapter Fifteen - Discovering America 115
Chapter Sixteen - Academic Doldrums 121
Chapter Seventeen - Sister Search 127
Chapter Eighteen - Getting By 133
Chapter Nineteen - Family Failings 141
Chapter Twenty - Money Matters 145
Chapter Twenty One - Naval Maneuvers 153
Chapter Twenty Two - Another Goodbye 161
Chapter Twenty Three - I Can Make It 165
Epilogue 177
Photo Gallery 180
About the Author 195

List of Illustrations

1. The Church in Timmervik 180
2. Edwin J. Vikman's Graduation Portrait 180
3. Hilma Carlson Vikman, Mother of Ed and Duane. 181
4. J. Arvid and Edwin J. Vikman 181
5. Ed and Duane with Father in Genoa 182
6. Portrait of Huldah Vikman 182
7. Aunt Huldah with Ed and Duane 183
8. Alice and Ruth with Ed and Duane 183
9. Ed and Duane in Genoa 184
10. Ed and "Dad" in Winnipeg 184
11. Ruth, Alice, Ed, and Duane in Holdrege 185
12. Ed and Duane at Edna Nelson's Farm 185
13. The House in Edmonton, Alberta 186
14. Family Portrait 186
15. Ed and Duane with the Carlson Family Dog 187
16. A Snow Cave 187
17. Ed and Duane with Classmates 188
18. The Washing Machine 188
19. The Separator 189
20. The Stone Boat 189
21. Ed and Duane with Farm Wagon 190
22. Duane with Hornet Stings 190
23. Ed and Duane with the Carlson Family 191
24. Ed and Duane with Confirmation Class 191
25. Ed and Duane's Confirmation Portrait 192
26. Ed and Duane in Hawaii 192
27. Ed and Duane's Picture in Edmonton Newspaper 193
28. Ed and Duane in the Garden 193
29. Portrait of Nancy and Ed 194

Prologue

The Augustana Lutheran Church in America* has a distinguished heritage enriched by the tradition of recording its history for future generations. This custom of archiving materials dates from the mid-nineteenth century, when the Augustana Synod was formed by gathering together and organizing Swedish immigrants who shared common traditions from the old country, particularly Lutheran liturgy and catechism.

Another great legacy of the Augustana Lutheran Church is the number of renowned liberal arts colleges and universities that it established throughout the United States, including Augustana College and Theological Seminary in Rock Island, Illinois, and Gustavus Adolphus College in St. Peter, Minnesota.

L. Dale Lund, PhD, a distinguished alumnus of these institutions and a past president of Bethany College in Lindsborg, Kansas, also established by the Augustana Lutheran Church, combined these two disciplines of academia and literature when he wrote a definitive history entitled *Partners in Mission 1962–1987: The Lutheran Church in America in Nebraska.* Pastor Lund, however, was more than a historian of fact and detail; he was a student of human nature as well. A handsome, white-haired gentleman, he had the kind of eyes that penetrated falsehood and illuminated goodness. He had caring eyes. With his humanistic interest, he frequently delved beneath the cold litany of births and deaths in the church registries and the record of pastoral accomplishments or the development of parish societies to enrich his research. He enjoyed the warmth of the weekly bulletins that detailed more intimately the lives of the clergy and their parishioners and enlivened the factual data.

On a visit to his son, Kent, in Denver, Colorado, he began to share some anecdotes he had collected while researching his materials. "One story has stayed with me all these years," he mused as he recounted the tragedy of a young family torn apart by illness and an automobile accident that orphaned fifteen-month-old twin boys. "It is one of the mysteries of the human condition," he added, "how men and women handle bereavement." He paused and said, "The twins were so young when it all happened. I've always wondered what became of those two little boys."

Smiling, Kent replied, "I think I can help you out. One of them is a client of mine, and I'm sure he'd like to tell you his story."

n.b. Pastor Lund died in 2012.

*The Augustana Lutheran Church ceased its existence when the Lutheran Church in America (LCA) was formed via a merger of several Lutheran synods, including Augustana, in 1962. With the addition of other synods in 1987, the Evangelical Lutheran Church of America (ECLA) was formed.

Acknowledgments

Just as Ed Vikman needed the support of his twin, Duane, to forge ahead and succeed in his early years, so did I need the encouragement, advice, and direction of many others in writing his story. It became apparent to me early on that I would depend on others to direct my research efforts. Many thanks to Suzanne Kaller, Reference Librarian, Denver Library District, Centennial, Colorado, who met with me on several occasions and suggested lines of investigation I needed to follow to corroborate Ed's memories. Suzanne's assistance taught me useful lessons about available Internet tools in addition to providing sources of information for medical, legal, and statistical records. I was constantly amazed at the goodwill and generosity of people I contacted and want to specifically thank Crista Santiapillai of Statistics Canada; Laura Neilson Bonikowsky, associate editor, The Canadian Encyclopedia, Historica Dominion Institute; and Andrea Faling, Head of Reference, Nebraska State Historical Society. All responded immediately and graciously to my email requests. Sandra B. Placzek, Associate Director, Schmid Law Library, University of Nebraska College of Law, provided key information on statutes regarding both midwifery and adoption during the 1930s. Sherry Bell, BA, Sp. (Cdn. Studies), MLIS, Reference Archivist, City of Edmonton Archives, introduced me to local history websites as well as *Edmonton in Our Own Words* by Linda Goyette and Carolina Jakeway Roemmich, a treasury of community lore and facts. Roberta Sohrweid, who grew up in Genoa, Nebraska, helped with background on life in her community. I owe Kent Lund thanks for biographical information he provided about his father, L. Dale Lund, PhD, and Rev. Charles Berdahl, DMin, friend and advisor, for his thoughtful insights and interpretations of Lutheran theology and practice.

A thousand thanks for always being with me go to my daughter, Julia Treacy Thompson, whose proofing skills and editorial suggestions and comments helped shape this manuscript; to Sosanna Kuruvila, whose support and understanding of a writer's blocks and pitfalls kept me going; to Nancy Vikman for her careful reading of the book and her delicious lunches while I interviewed her husband; and to Elizabeth Victoria Wallace who introduced me to Ed Vikman as well as to my editor.

Joan W. Sherman, editor par excellence, provided unerring recommendations and suggestions to bring this book to a high level of professionalism. She recognized and clarified passages and characterizations that would have only confused the reader. She gave me only the most positive reinforcement and truly made me feel like a writer.

Lastly, I want to thank Edwin T. Vikman, whose courage, values and dreams were the impetus for this, my first book.

Sadly, Ed died on May 7, 2013, before the publication of his memoir, but he read and approved the manuscript before his death.

Chronology

March 19, 1931	Ed and Duane Vikman are born in Genoa, Nebraska
March 31, 1931	Hilma Vikman, mother, dies after childbirth
June 28, 1932	Rev. Edwin J. Vikman, father, dies in auto accident
August 1932	Ed and Duane move to Winnipeg, Manitoba to live with Uncle Arvid "Dad" and Aunt Hildore
Mid-August 1932–November 1935	Ed and Duane live with Aunt Huldah in Sweden
Midwinter 1935–1936	Ed and Duane return to the United States and live in Holdrege, Nebraska, with maternal grandparents
1936–1938	Ed and Duane live with their Aunt Hildore and Uncle Arvid Vikman in Saskatoon and Regina, Saskatchewan and occasional foster families
1938–1939	Ed and Duane live on Aunt Edna Nelson's farm, in Axtell, Nebraska
1939	Dad purchases home in Edmonton, Alberta
1939	Ed and Duane live in Fort Saskatchewan, Alberta, with Grandahl family
1940–1943	With a home base in Edmonton, Ed and Duane live with various foster families

1943–1945	Ed and Duane live on the Carlsons' farm
1946	Ed and Duane return to Nebraska, and Ed works on the farm in Beaver City
1946–1950	Ed and Duane attend Luther Academy in Wahoo, Nebraska
1950	Duane enlists in the U.S. Navy after graduation from Luther Academy
1951	Ed attends Luther College for part of a year and then enlists in the U.S. Navy
1954–1962	Ed returns to civilian life as a student and begins his career
1962	Ed becomes a permanent resident of Denver, Colorado
October 12, 1979	Ed and Nancy marry
May 7, 2013	Ed Vikman dies

Family and Associates of Ed and Duane Vikman

Hilma and Edwin J. Vikman	Parents
Ruth Vikman Johnson	Sister
Alice Vikman Christianson	Sister
Claus G. and Augusta B. Carlson	Maternal Grandparents
Carl V. T. Carlson	Maternal Uncle
Phillip Carlson	First cousin, son of Carl
Anna Carlson Hassel	Maternal Aunt
J. Arvid Vikman	Paternal Uncle
Hildore (Mrs. Arvid) Vikman	Paternal aunt by marriage
Huldah Vikman	Paternal Aunt
Miriam Vikman	First cousin, daughter of Arvid
Linnea Vikman	First cousin, daughter of Arvid
Edna Nelson	Sister of Hildore Vikman
Effie Nelson	Cousin of Hildore Vikman

Families Employing Ed and Duane Vikman

Ted Grandahl	Fort Saskatchewan, Alberta
Gus and Ellen Larson	Edmonton, Alberta
The Tennis Family	Meeting Creek, Alberta
Fritz Johansen	Near Edmonton, Alberta
Theo & Elna Carlson (no relation)	Camrose, Alberta
Clifford, Florene, Cecelia, Raymond	Children of Theodore and Elna

A Few Supportive Friends

Einar Carlson	Parishioner who befriended Ed and Duane
Hildur and Astrid Carlson	Sisters of Einar and party hosts during Ed's leave in Edmonton
Alfrida Benson	Landlady in Wahoo, Nebraska
Shirley Dean and Nora Moffat	Early Edmonton allies

Introduction

My name is Edwin T. Vikman and now, in 2013, I am eighty-two years old. I've had a good life since I became old enough to manage it myself, but I am still trying to understand the events of my childhood. Then, I walked in the direction the adult finger pointed. Usually, it was not a happy destination.

Recently, as I wandered past the landscapes at a local art gallery, I expected to see myself in the canvases because the scenes looked so familiar. They reminded me of my life long ago on the farm in Canada where my twin, Duane, and I had been forced to labor starting at the age of eleven. One painting brought memories of the sharp sting of sleet as I battled my way across the frozen yard from the decrepit house to the dilapidated old barn each morning before dawn during the long winter months. With the next painting, I remembered the ache in my chest as I staggered into the wind that blew drifts of snow across the fields. The faded stain on the ramshackle shed in this painting resembled the color of the outbuilding where we milked the cows before school. The two draft horses whose shaggy coats barely concealed their muscular strength might have been Jerry and Fly, the dappled grays that Duane and I used to harness on the farm in Alberta. Those horses were big and old and probably not very smart, but they were good and dependable and worked as hard as we did. They were almost the only friends we had on that farm. As I gazed at the pictures hanging in the museum, I was grateful for the warmth of my favorite tweed jacket and the lifetime that separated me from the cruel memories these images evoked. Those early years weren't good ones, but I got through them. I learned the mantra that has sustained me for eight decades: "If I don't dream now, 'I can make it!' I won't even come close."

As Duane and I were growing up, we encountered many obstacles to happiness as well as material success. We frequently lived in unspeakable conditions, we wore secondhand clothes that were old-fashioned or much too small or too large, we lacked nutritious meals and received no medical attention. As boys, we worked long hours doing men's work and were paid nothing. Our physical struggles, moreover, were matched by the emotional hardships we endured. Worst of all, I don't ever remember anyone saying, "I love you, Ed."

I've heard of other boys whose childhoods included similar years of misery, but all too often such stories are told by grown men as a prelude to why they drink too much, or spend half their lives in prison, or why they think they deserve a monthly welfare check. I am sorry for those men, but I think most of them didn't have to end their lives that way. As a child I discovered deep wells of courage and faith within myself that helped me see beyond the anger and meanness I met almost every day. I learned that there were two ways to approach every difficulty: I could sit on the curb outside my house and cry, or I could see the rainbow in the puddles at my feet. It wasn't always easy, but I want readers to understand from my experiences that with optimism and a lot of hard work, most people can become productive and achieve many of their goals. I recently saw a report about the success rates of children who had grown up in disadvantaged situations. I found it fascinating to see the conclusions reached that neither the test grades nor the schools the students attended determined their success as adults. Rather, it was the resilience they exhibited as they overcame their problems. It was the optimists who won the race and took home the prize; the pessimists dropped by the wayside. I found myself nodding my head as I read this. It is the story of my life, the story I want to tell to convince others that they don't have to give up. It doesn't matter if your childhood is rotten or life treats you unfairly. It matters only that you hold tight to hope and feed your dreams. That's how I achieved happiness in my work and love in my life and proved that misfortune didn't need to be the pattern I had to follow.

But maybe I'm getting ahead of myself, and I should tell you more about my life, what it was like for me growing up, and how my brother and I got to that farm.

Duane and I became orphans when we were just fifteen months old, and from that moment we embarked on a journey of constant change. Twelve days after our birth, our mother was rushed to the hospital after our home delivery, and she died after hemorrhaging severely. When our father then died unexpectedly in an automobile accident, we went to live with his brother and family in Canada; we also spent two years with our Aunt Huldah in

Sweden while our uncle studied for an advanced degree there. Those years with her were the only completely happy ones of our childhood. After we returned to Manitoba, Duane and I were treated badly by relatives who should have been our greatest protectors. Nobody wanted us to live with them—I don't know why most of them were so mean to us. We never did anything to hurt anybody. We were just two defenseless boys who wanted to grow up and be loved.

Shortly after our fifth birthday, our uncle, who insisted that we call him Dad, (although, as you will learn, we didn't call his wife Mom) sent us away to a home where we didn't know anyone. After that, we continued to live with strangers during most of our childhood. Unfortunately, when we lived with our closest relatives we received some of the worst treatment we ever experienced. That hurt us the most because we realized those were the people who should really have cared for us. Those who should have hugged us tight held us at arm's length. I'm still not sure why.

The only real certainties I have about my early life relate to the deaths of my parents and the hardships my brother and I endured. The greatest certainty I have about my life today, though, is that I dared to dream I would make it, and I did.

First, however, we grappled with the realization that to survive emotionally we had to rely on each other. Even when we were too young to put the thoughts into words, we learned to bounce all our ideas off each another. I was the firstborn twin, but we were always two halves of the whole. Like most identical twins, we looked so much alike that people frequently confused us, but those who knew us best could see that Duane's ears were just slightly larger than mine. In pictures, he is also identifiable by the slight curve in the way he holds his right arm. But those differences paled in importance to the strength of our mutual support in growing up.

Fortunately, someone—I think it might have been one of our sisters—kept snapshots of our early years together, and those photos invariably show us close together, held in our father's arms, or side by side in the carriage, or posed side by side in a chair. Biologically we were identical twins, the product of one original egg at fertilization, and psychologically we recognized our other half—the person who would never disappoint or let us down.

Before I elaborate further, let me tell you about my family and the events that led to the torments of our early life. My parents, Hilma and Pastor Edwin J. Vikman, lived in the parsonage next to the Augustana Lutheran Church on

Webster Street in the heart of Genoa, Nebraska, with our sisters Ruth and Alice. They had lived in the town of about twelve hundred people since 1929.

My father came to America from Sweden in 1902 at the age of eighteen, hoping, like most immigrants of the time, to discover a pot of gold or at least a secure future. His last name at that time was Josephsson. At Ellis Island he changed his name to Johnson because it sounded more American. Later, after he was ordained a minister, he changed it to Vikman. I'm not sure why he made that change, but I would imagine he realized there were just too many people named Johnson. A more unusual surname would help him to stand out. I was told he formed his new name from the last syllable of the town Timmervik in Sweden where he had been confirmed and where some of his family had lived, and he added the word *man*.

Once when I was going through an old family album, I found a picture of the church in Timmervik. It looked attractive to me with its tall ivy-covered steeple with a cross on it and a little cemetery in front guarded by a wrought iron railing. I have often wondered if any of my ancestors are buried there.

My father had been working in a factory in Jamestown, New York, when he felt the call from God to enter His service in the ministry. He visited his pastor, who encouraged him to follow his vocation, and in 1909 he entered Augustana College and Theological Seminary in Rock Island, Illinois, where he met my mother. She was studying at the Conservatory of Music. They married in 1920.

After his ordination in 1919 at Lindsborg, Kansas, my father was assigned to the Swinner-White Stone Hill Parish in North Dakota. He then became pastor at churches in Axtell, Nebraska, and Lake Lillian, Minnesota, before he and my mother went to Genoa, Nebraska.

A group of Mormons had founded Genoa on their trek west. By the time my parents arrived, it had been home to a Lutheran congregation since 1910. It was still the early years of the Great Depression, the almost decade-long period of high unemployment and scant wages that started with the Wall Street crash in 1928. Drought had begun to envelop the countryside, but just as that devastating phenomenon was going to grow and smother the land, our family was soon going to experience a black blizzard of its own and an emotional turmoil that would affect us as no dust bowl could.

Chapter One
The Last Christmas

I never knew my parents, but I've often wondered what they were like. I know some general details from the newspaper accounts I have about their marriage and their deaths and from the few memories my sisters have shared. That's all I know for sure. I've read a little bit about life in the 1930s, and once I met a woman who also lived in Genoa at the time we were born. She told me stories she had heard from her mother, and she also shared some of her own memories. I've imagined a lot of the rest, perhaps because I needed to create the mother I never knew.

I think it was probably a bit of a shock when our mother learned she was having her third baby, and as it turned out, it was actually my twin brother and me. She was already thirty-seven years old and weighed down by the responsibilities of raising two young daughters, all the while attending to the church suppers, fetes and innumerable tasks expected of a pastor's wife. She also played the church organ and led the choir. Despite being a great musician, she still had to practice the hymns during the week for each Sunday's services. She was a busy woman, but she nonetheless set aside time each day to read her Bible. From what my father wrote about her in the issue of *The Church Herald* after her death, she relished the time she could spend at prayer to develop her special relationship with the Lord. Her deep faith was her greatest legacy to her children.

I think my mother must have felt quite tired when her alarm clock rang early in the mornings as her pregnancy advanced, and I'm sure the additional bulk she was carrying made her chores much more difficult and tiring. I imagine her days seemed very long to her. Each week she would have to scrub the clothing and linens in large galvanized tubs, rub out the stubborn stains on the washboard, and feed the sodden laundry through the wringer before dragging it up the basement steps to the clothes line to dry. "Lord, give me strength," she probably prayed. (As I've mentioned, she was close to Jesus, whom she called her *Savior.*)

"Ruth and I tried so hard to help her," Alice told me many years later. "We set the table for dinner, and we peeled never-ending sacks of potatoes, but we couldn't seem to make a dent in all the things there were to do." By then my sisters were old enough to assume many household tasks like making their own beds, but in those days before permanent press and frozen foods and microwaves, keeping a family fed and clothed was a heavy-duty task.

Nevertheless, our mother insisted they still needed to enjoy their childhood, and she encouraged them to join their youth groups at the church. She liked to help out at those meetings, where she could silently observe her daughters and enjoy their accomplishments.

"Let them go do their homework," my sisters heard her say, when our dad scolded that she needed to rest more. "They'll grow up soon enough," she would add. Mother apparently liked to think of them still as little girls. It must have amused her to hear Ruth, only ten years old, proclaiming, "But Mother, soon I'll be grownup!" Alice, at seven, still played with her old paper dolls, although only when she thought no one would notice. Some people thought the girls resembled Mother.

Christmas 1930 came, with all the extra choir rehearsals for the midnight service and Ruth and Alice helping to bake the St. Lucia buns and the gingerbread men. Everyone decorated the tree with the colorful glass balls they had cherished for years. Some of the ornaments were so heavy they could only be hung on the bottom branches. I can almost hear them laughing as they pricked their fingers on the needles while stringing popcorn and cranberries for garlands. I wish I could have seen them as they discovered the favorites remembered from past holidays. Ruth later described making paper chains every year, since no matter how carefully they wrapped them as they packed them away, they always looked too forlorn the following season to use them. Some of the neighbors had begun to string electric lights on their trees, but Ruth told me at another time how glad Mother was that our father still preferred to use real candles. It took him quite a while to fasten the short tapers to the tips of each branch with melted wax, making sure there was enough space for the flame to burn without catching the needles above. I've seen pictures of trees like that, and they seem to glow in a special way that's different from electricity. Of course, my father would have kept buckets of water nearby just in case there was a fire.

The girls carefully eyed the packages that Mother brought out from her hiding places to tuck under the tree, but they knew better than to shake them or poke them with curious fingers. They didn't really want to know what was in them before Christmas. Another treat was listening to the stories our father told and the traditions he recalled from his early years in Sweden. Finally, before Mother became so exhausted she almost fell asleep in her chair, she would bring in a plate laden with her favorite marzipan candies dipped in bittersweet chocolate a friend sent every year from Sweden. She always included *knäck*, a chewy toffee made from sugar, syrup and cream for Ruth, but Alice, with the sweetest tooth in the family, preferred *ischoklad*, a soft chocolate candy that melts in your mouth. Everyone knew our father liked his *lakrits* which I think is the best licorice in the world.

Despite her pregnancy and fatigue, Mother would have spent hours ironing the napkins and tablecloths from her trousseau, having first aired them carefully after removing them from her hope chest. The fragrance of the cedar lining must have smelled wonderful to her when she lifted the lid. She polished her best silverware and crystal and admired them again as she did each holiday season. Some day she would enjoy giving them to her children.

Everything took so much longer to accomplish when her hands and feet were swollen and stiff. This pregnancy must have seemed more difficult than her earlier ones, especially since she had been a lot younger! Ruth remembers the family and their friends were becoming anxious for the remaining months to pass quickly, especially since our mother was beginning to look like she might be carrying twins. But in the meantime, December 25th was coming quickly, and celebrating in the Swedish tradition meant much baking and cooking for Mother. She prepared the rich cream sauce for the herring and the customary boiled potatoes and the delicious potato sausage. The family always devoured the thick custard at dessert and never left a crumb from the coffeecake studded with plump raisins and almonds. She liked to have extra meatballs and gravy to serve with tart lingonberry jam as they did in Sweden and saved pickled beets for the next day, so she wouldn't have to cook again.

Our father was usually so preoccupied with preparing his sermon for the midnight service and worrying that everything would sound just right that he didn't always appreciate the Christmas Eve feast as much as he might. He was usually hungrier the next day when he could finally rest after they had opened their presents.

My sisters found new sweaters Mother had knit when they tore the wrappings off the next morning. Alice spent the rest of the day playing with her new Uncle Wiggly board game, while Ruth studied the rules of her chess set. Mother finally had her long awaited chance to take a nap and even read part of the new Agatha Christie whodunit she had received from her mother. Many years later, Alice said she remembered almost every minute of that Christmas celebration, the last one she had with our mother—Mother's last Christmas.

January and February passed, and when March arrived, it was time for the final preparations for the delivery. My parents had decided that this time Mother would give birth at home. It was a mistake, but no one would realize that until it was too late.

Several of the neighbors in Genoa had recently had home deliveries, and they had raved about how much more intimate it seemed than giving birth in the cold sterility of the maternity ward. It also seemed sensible with the unpredictability of late winter snowstorms, when the roads could be totally impassable or the old car didn't want to start. It was too bad there wasn't enough money to buy one of those elegant silver Buick Eights that was advertised in the *Saturday Evening Post*, but such a purchase wasn't possible on a pastor's salary.

Putting daydreams aside, she would get back to the cake she was making for the sewing circle or the darning that awaited in a pile of socks. The girls were adept now at replacing the buttons on their blouses, but they hadn't yet mastered the delicate task of repairing their hose without the little knots or bumps that resulted in painful blisters. To be sure, Pastor Vikman was not only handsome but also very reasonable—but no one wanted to limp around all day because there were lumps in his socks!

My mother collected all the items they would need for the delivery—the extra sheets and bed pads, towels and wash cloths, a bucket, and hot water bottles. The list seemed endless, but she checked off each item systematically. She thanked God daily that she would have dear Mrs. Haber, the midwife, in attendance. Mrs. H. had assisted many of the church ladies in their deliveries, so it was reassuring to know she would be there. She seemed so gentle when she coached Mother on how she would help.

Mother had invited her own mother to come although Grandma was getting old. It would be good just to have her there to hold her hand and keep Edwin out of the bedroom until it was all over. If Mother dared admit it to herself, the prospect of birthing two babies was frightening.

The morning finally came when she awoke with the telltale cramps announcing her labor had begun. For a moment she must have felt nervous when she remembered the calm efficiency of the hospital staff when the girls were born and then looked around at the familiar roses on the bedroom wallpaper instead. In that first morning light, I wonder if Mother regretted her earlier decision and if she missed hearing the starched rustle of the nurse's uniforms and seeing the perky caps atop their netted hair. Whispering her favorite prayer, "Jesus, remember me," and hearing the voices of our grandmother and the midwife who had performed this duty many times before, hopefully lulled her back to sleep.

But that morning would be tragically different from those other days when Ruth and Alice were born. This delivery was both lengthy and difficult, and she hemorrhaged badly. Finally, after many hours, Duane and I were born to an exhausted mother who would never recover.

Unfortunately, neither the midwife, nor my grandmother, nor my father realized the injuries my mother suffered during childbirth. Twelve days later she was transferred to the hospital in Columbus, Nebraska. There, after much consultation among the doctors as the family hovered close by, they reached the decision to try a blood transfusion.

Although blood typing had been known to the medical world for over thirty years, not much was known about storing blood, and there were no blood banks anywhere in the United States. Transfusions were still risky, particularly in small rural hospitals, but it seemed the doctor thought a transfusion would be the only way to save Mother's life. Later, my sister told me that she might have been given the wrong blood type because, according to the newspaper account of her death, she died just a few hours after the transfusion. It was 8:00 p.m. on Tuesday, March 31, 1931. She was buried three days later, on Good Friday, in the cemetery in Holdrege, Nebraska.

Our father baptized us Theodore Edwin and Duane Gustav in the parsonage after the funeral. Our sisters don't remember anything else about that day except how silent everything seemed. Quietly they dragged their feet as they crossed the path from the brick church, overcrowded with mourners, to the chill of the empty manse. The ladies' guild had surpassed its usual hospitality as they comforted the pastor and his family and plied the visiting dignitaries with casseroles and sandwiches and finger cakes, but the moment had come, as it always does, to go home. Exhaustion lined everyone's faces, but my father had one more sacramental duty to perform. We know again from the church bulletin, that our mother had received Holy Communion just a few days before she died and had told our father, "Jesus fills the whole room." He knew that one of her last wishes would be for him to baptize us as soon as possible, but by now his church probably held too much sorrow for him. Perhaps, he just needed to escape the dolorous notes of the organ and the cloying scent of the flowers; maybe he wanted to be alone with his two motherless daughters and twin boys. Whatever his reasons, he brought us into his beloved Lutheran church in the simplicity of our home.

Chapter Two
Sons No More

Our father was just a few days short of his forty-eighth birthday when our mother died, and accomplished as he was as a pastor and counselor to his congregation, nothing in his life had prepared him to be both father and mother to his growing brood. He wrote to his sister Huldah, who lived in Sweden, and asked her to come to America to help with us. Once our father's need was clear to her, she abandoned a lucrative nursing career and soon arrived in Nebraska.

One of the earliest pictures we have shows our dad cradling us, one in each arm, as he stood in the garden of the dark green clapboard parsonage where we lived during that sad spring. In another photo, Ruth and Alice, grinning broadly, and looking every inch the big sisters, flank us on the narrow path weaving past the house. Anyone passing by would probably have described us as a contented family, thinking it was our mother who was the photographer and not Aunt Huldah—Dad looks incredibly serene. Even when we outgrew his embrace and were photographed sitting on our small tricycles, he always had his arms protectively around the two of us. Another of my favorite pictures shows Aunt Huldah, clad in a fur-trimmed coat and matching hat, reaching out, eager to be another pair of hands to cuddle us. It is clear we were surrounded by an aura of love at that point in our lives.

Aunt Huldah had a lot of juggling to do as she adjusted from being a single woman to being the manager of a large, busy household. She had left many friends and activities in her native Sweden, where she had also held a successful position as a hospital nurse, and she was used to a much livelier ambience than she found in small-town Genoa. "But I have always enjoyed a challenge," she confided to our maternal grandmother, Augusta Carlson. "I think Edwin and the children and I will adjust to one another with a little time."

Aunt Huldah could read and write English fluently, but she sometimes had difficulty in conversation, and she occasionally felt left out of the gossip when she was with the ladies' groups at church. "I can order from the butcher all right, but I do wish I could understand American jokes," she remarked a little wistfully. Nevertheless, she determined to keep the household running just as smoothly as it had in her sister-in-law's day, even though the home now included two baby boys. Months later, on June 28, 1932, her early success shattered when our father died in a car crash.

Alice told me when I was grown that she had vivid memories of that day. The morning started much like any other except for the excitement my sisters felt as they prepared for a special treat. They were going with Father to attend a district meeting of the Women's Missionary Society in Hordville, Nebraska, where the Fridhem Lutheran church had been erected in 1882. Participants would be coming from miles around, and my sisters anticipated meeting new girls their age. It was almost a half day's drive on country roads.

For such an important occasion, Ruth wore the brooch Mother used to pin to her best Sunday outfit and the new flowered dress with the double flounced skirt that she had just bought at the dress shop in town. Alice had a brand-new hair ribbon she had been saving especially for the occasion and Aunt Huldah had added trim to a hand-me-down of Ruth's. The girls had carefully ironed their outfits the night before and were up early to help with breakfast.

On this day, three other women and another young girl would be with them in the car. The tan Nash, manufactured in Kenosha, Wisconsin, had two folding seats in the back that could easily accommodate the younger passengers. Unfortunately, the innovative motor company would not invent the seatbelt until 1949.

With light hearts and maybe even singing a song or a hymn or two, the group set out from Genoa. The roads leading from the small town were paved at first, but soon gave way to gravel as the Nash passed the outskirts of town and headed from Nance County, south on Highway K-N-D, to Hamilton County. Acres of corn and grain crowded the fields, growing almost to the edge of the road and limiting visibility for drivers as they passed by. As Father reached the intersection at White Way, a Studebaker heading west to Loup City approached, and each driver, apparently not seeing the other, continued into the crossroads past the "slow" signs. The sheriff's office determined later that both cars were proceeding at speeds higher than the posted 45 mph limit. A screech of brakes and the sounds of shattering headlights reverberated throughout the countryside as the two vehicles collided. The Studebaker slammed broadside into the Nash sending both cars crashing into a nearby ditch.

Walter Gagle, son of the owner of the filling station on the far corner, witnessed the impact, and his reports revealed important details of the accident. All he could see at first, he told the policeman who wrote out the accident report, were the cars with wheels still spinning and the figure of a man, clad in a gray suit, lying on the ground. The June 30, 1932, issue of the *Central City News* reported that "[the cars] burst into flames before the dust had been blown away."

Walter, joined by his father, Dave, who was working in a nearby field, rushed over to the devastating scene. Cries of fright from the dazed passengers assaulted the men's ears as they helped them from the crumpled wreck. Fire was already spreading from the hood of the Nash toward the passenger seats. The *News* noted that "only the heroic work of the Gagles saved the ladies from further horror. Just a few of them would have been able to extricate themselves."

All six of the women and girls in Pastor Vikman's car, as well as the driver and her daughter in the other car, received cuts and bruises. Dr. Earl E. Boyd administered first aid at the scene and then took these individuals to his office in town for further treatment. The youngest, it was discovered, suffered a fracture at the base of her skull. For several days doctors were afraid her injury might be fatal.

In their disoriented state immediately after the crash, Ruth and Alice at first saw only the legs and lower body of Father's prone figure. "He looked like he was sleeping," Alice said when she told me the whole story many years later. Other passersby reported that he lay rolled up by the car, with traumatic injuries to his head and face. He had died instantly.

At the doctor's office where the women and girls were all taken, cots filled the reception room and the patients' examining rooms. News accounts reported that Dr. Boyd and four nurses attended to the injured passengers.

My sisters, of course, were traumatized by the accident and their continued separation from Father. After their wounds had been cleaned and dressed and the women had succeeded in calming them, Dr. Boyd told Ruth and Alice that Father was dead. His body had already been taken to the funeral home.

The news account indicated that the age-old problem of right-of-way was likely the fundamental cause of the tragedy, in addition to speed. It was also suggested that since this was the second collision at that intersection, stop signs should be erected there.

Two days later, funeral services were conducted in Genoa, with several members of the Lutheran clergy participating. A minister from Axtell, Nebraska, read a passage from Luke, and Mother's brother, Uncle Carl, sang a solo, "Be Still and Know." He had also sung at our mother and father's wedding. The theme of the sermon centered on "thy brother shall rise again," as spoken by Jesus to Mary and Martha in the New Testament. Dr. C. O. Gulleen delivered the sermon.

Father's body was then taken to Holdrege, and additional services were held in the church there before he was interred next to our mother in Prairie Home Cemetery. Pastors of both churches served as honorary pallbearers, while members of the church councils actually carried the casket.

The obituary printed in the September–October 1932 issue of *The Church Herald* in Genoa described Father as "a powerful preacher" and added that "an abundance of the Bible, hymns and spiritual songs, experience, and the warmest, serious and challenging fervor characterized his sermons and preaching." It praised him for his conviction that preaching should be more personal, encouraging the individual to explore his own relationship with God.

Fortunately, Duane and I later obtained other copies of the *Herald* that our father had edited and published at his earlier churches, so we know he wrote with a style that was spare in comparison to the prevailing fashion of the religious prose in the 1930s. During his pastorate at the First Lutheran Church in Lake Lillian, Minnesota, he referred to the monthly newsletter as the pastor's assistant in promoting the interest of the church and the community. When he spoke of the religious fervor of the community church he visited in Sweden, he commented that when people attended church in that country, there was no discussion of the wheat or stock market. He described the atmosphere, saying, "All was still; all was quiet. Their hearts were tuned for worship." No wonder Father was praised for his intellect and sincerity.

Now both my parents were dead. We had so few bits and pieces about them to know what they had really been like. Their years had been few, their lives unfinished homilies. How different ours might have been if the two people who loved us most had not died so prematurely. We had lost both our parents—we were sons no more.

At this time, my uncle officially changed my name from Theodore Edwin to Edwin T. Vikman in honor of our father.

Chapter Three
Unwanted

Once again my family descended on the small town of Genoa, but a dispute arose about what to do with the four of us children. My mother's parents, Mr. and Mrs. Claus Carlson of Holdrege, Nebraska, were already seventy-two and sixty respectively, but they agreed to take their granddaughters. "Ruth and Alice are old enough to help with the house," they told those gathered for the funeral, "but we're just too old to run after two little boys. Someone else will have to look after them." How cold those words seem now.

Other maternal relatives had gathered for the memorial services, but they also considered two budding toddlers an obstacle to their established way of life. Our mother's sister, Anna, and her husband, also named Carl, were childless, and they plainly indicated that they would object to any change in the status of their lives.

"The only solution," our mother's brother, Uncle Carl, told the assembled family, "is to place Duane and Edwin in Boys Town." He already had a four year old son, Phillip. "I've checked, and it's the only available orphanage that will take them." Father Edward J. Flanagan had established this still thriving community for homeless boys near Omaha, Nebraska, in 1921.

Our father's brother, Arvid, the man we later called "Dad," also a Lutheran minister, could not agree. "I can't leave these boys to be brought up in a Catholic institution," he stated, not realizing that even then the home accepted children without regard to race, color or creed. With that ultimatum on the table, he decided to take us back to Winnipeg to join his wife, Hildore, and their two daughters, Miriam and Linnea, who were sixteen months and twenty-seven months, respectively.

Before that happened, however, Uncle Carl, my mother's brother, decided, as executor of the wills, he would sell everything my parents had owned. I wonder how my mother would have liked that. I have a copy of the newspaper account of my parents' wedding that describes all the useful and beautiful gifts my parents were given. I wish, now, that I had some of their crystal and china; even as an elderly man, I would treasure things they had used and touched.

I think I might have felt closer to my parents if I had known what they liked and been given the opportunity to use some of their belongings. Now all I have is a few pictures of the two of them and a handful of postcards and letters, mementos even Uncle Carl couldn't sell. I think now that greed motivated the sale, and that he hoped to use the money for himself, but if that was his true intent, he never in fact profited. We learned when we were almost grown, however, that he succeeded in losing our rightful inheritance in other ways. As it turned out, Duane and I would eventually derive some benefit from our parents' estate, but there would be many bumps in the road of our lives before that occurred.

Since I never knew my parents, my stories about them are largely derived from my imagination and from talking to my sisters. I'm not sure if I was ever placed on my mother's chest to be held or cuddled before she died. I'm certain, though, that my father was loving and affectionate— the family photos show that—but, unfortunately, I was too young to retain such wonderful memories. The early photographs of us with our father reveal his gentleness and the pride he took in his two sons as he did his best to be both mother and father to us. His protective arms seem to be guarding us from the world.

Duane and I experienced little affection once we went back to Canada with Uncle Arvid, despite the fact that he liked it when we called him Dad. Unfortunately, Aunt Huldah had returned to Sweden and would not care for us again until Dad brought us there shortly after we joined his family.

I must have experienced a rich love in the fifteen months we had with our father and during the preceding nine months when I had lived under my mother's heart. We know now that babies in the womb can not only hear but also can recognize noises and often react sharply to intrusive sounds, just as they will gently kick when they hear a familiar voice. How amazing to think that what I sensed even before I came into the world may have significantly influenced my ability to reach beyond the moment and believe in the future. Perhaps in some mysterious way that was when my hopes were born.

Psychologists tell us that feelings are developed before children are even two years old. Somehow, from our birth until our father's death, Duane and I had to have known deep love, because I have always experienced warmth for other people even in my bleakest circumstances.

Aunt Hildore thought that having us move in with them was an unforgivable intrusion, but she had to accept Dad's decision. Fortunately, during August, shortly after our arrival in Canada, we all sailed for Sweden on the Swedish American liner Drottningholm. Dad had made plans the previous year to continue his studies at the University of Uppsala and to visit his aging mother. It must have been a terrible time for my grandmother, losing a son she hadn't seen since his marriage and not being able to attend his funeral and say good-bye.

The plans suited Aunt Hildore perfectly since they presented her with a solution to having us under foot. She arranged for Duane and me to be reunited with Aunt Huldah and to live with her for the next few years until our return to Canada on another Swedish American ship, the Gripsholm, in 1935.

My memories of our time in Sweden are understandably minimal, but I recall one incident at Aunt Huldah's that showed what a kind mother figure she was to us. Duane and I saw what we thought was a small flock of crows in Aunt Huldah's yard. We must have believed they would eat the vegetables she was so carefully tending in her garden because we ran among them yelling, "shoo, shoo," hoping they would fly away. Instead, we accidentally stepped on a couple of them, killing them. When we confessed this to Aunt Huldah, she merely sighed, "You've killed my chickens," and didn't reprimand us further. She didn't scold that these were her prize bantee hens and important layers of eggs for the household.

Duane and I had already experienced Aunt Hildore's unreasonable anger when we exhibited normal little boy antics or misbehaviors during our short time with her, so Aunt Huldah's response to our unwitting error soothed me. I think, young as I was, I already understood the difference between Aunt Hildore's rejection and Aunt Huldah's affection and was comforted by the latter's indulgence. I feel confident that Aunt Huldah's early warmth nourished the seed planted by my parents' love. Early photos of her, as well, reflect the love she had for all her nieces and nephews.

What would our childhood have been like if Dad had stuck to his original plan of having us stay in Sweden when he returned to Canada? How strange that he didn't consider a Catholic orphanage or a spinster aunt as proper guardians, but would later send us to live with people he knew almost nothing about, after we were completely rejected by Aunt Hildore.

When we returned from Sweden, at age five, we first went to visit our grandparents in Holdrege, Nebraska, where Ruth and Alice had been living.

Life felt confining at times for them, and they had faced some difficult years of adjustment. Just when my sisters should have been exploring new ideas and trying their wings as emerging adolescents, they had to conform to the set pattern the elder Carlsons had established.

It was hard for Grandmother Carlson to understand how important it was, particularly for Ruth, to wear the latest fashions and read the newest magazines. She had probably forgotten she had faced the same challenges when she was raising our mother. As so often happens, Grandmother was sure this younger generation was much too permissive, but she knew the girls sometimes chafed under her strict rules. She didn't really like the pictures in the new teen magazine *YM* and wasn't sure that Nancy Drew was just the right role model for her granddaughters. She had read one of the books when the girls were at school, and she didn't like learning about Nancy's boyfriend, Ned, or the little roadster she drove around town. She would have much preferred they entertained themselves with monopoly or checkers or the new game of Scrabble, but she didn't forbid them to read the book.

Of course, Ruth and Alice were much too young to have dates or to drive, but Grandmother wasn't sure she wanted them to be thinking about those things yet. So, when the girls learned we were returning from Sweden and begged to have us come for a visit, Grandmother thought it might be a good distraction for them. The interlopers wouldn't stay too long, she undoubtedly hoped.

About all we have from that special visit is a picture of our two older sisters and us two towheaded little boys, all smiling and staring straight ahead at the camera. The four of us wouldn't be together again for many, many years.

This makes it doubly unfortunate that we don't have any memories of our stay. I don't even have any recollection of saying goodbye to them. It was only after we had all grown to adulthood that we were able to piece together the story of our early lives and share our memories. By then, we all lived many miles apart, but, fortunately, had developed affectionate relationships with one another, and we enjoyed our visits.

The pattern that was going to characterize our youth, and which would eventually make us feel like outcasts, began to take shape when we left Holdrege. After returning from Sweden, we were again being uprooted from anything and anyone the least bit familiar when Dad sent us to live in Axtell, Nebraska, with Hildore's sister, Edna Nelson. We were only six years old, but we had already lived in Genoa, Nebraska; Winnipeg, Manitoba; Árbol

Sundals Ryr, Sweden; Holdrege, Nebraska; Regina and Saskatoon, Saskatchewan, as Dad struggled to support the family in small country parishes. Now, we were back once more in the United States. To make life even more unsettling for the two of us, several of those moves had also meant adjusting to the lifestyles of new sets of adults.

Looking back at that year with Edna, I think it was ok, although it might only have seemed that way in comparison to the life we soon faced. We had enough to eat and a bed to sleep in and, like Aunt Huldah, Edna seemed to enjoy our company. At least we had a mattress which covered the entire box spring, a luxury we would later miss when we had only a flimsy cloth covering on a metal bedstead and dark shadows instead of electricity. We could lie in bed and watch the dust motes dancing in the shafts of sunlight that woke us up and luxuriate in snuggling down again under the covers before heeding Aunt Edna's call to breakfast. The tantalizing aroma of country bacon at Edna Nelson's promised a bountiful repast for both of us—a start to the day we wouldn't enjoy again for years.

All too soon, in the cellar that became our home in Edmonton, Canada, we would awaken in the same suffocating blackness that had curled tentacles of terror around us before we escaped to sleep. Perhaps it's just as well we didn't know at the time that Axtell represented our last taste of the freedom to be little boys—boys who could revel in how high we could climb or how fast we could run into the breezes that tugged at our shirttails; we even basked in Aunt Edna's praise at how well we had learned to weed her vegetable plot. I'm not sure if Edna was a pretty woman, but her round cheeks crinkled with frequent smiles and, although her skirts were generally covered by an immaculate apron, she never minded if we burrowed our grimy faces into her lap. She must have had an inexhaustible store of clean replacements.

About the only grown up who had spent much time in conversation with us had been Aunt Huldah, and she, of course, especially while we lived with her, had spoken in Swedish. Dad addressed most of his remarks to us in his native language rather than English, so we really couldn't explain ourselves very well in our mother tongue. We had barely started to talk when we left Canada, and when we returned, the family continued to communicate as they had in Scandinavia.

As a result of this situation, I still don't know what Edna thought I said the day she became angry and washed my mouth out with the laundry soap. I tried to hide under the bed but she dragged me out, and I never said that word ever again. Our language difficulties would continue to plague us for many years and cause major problems for us in school. However, when we were much older, we would sometimes use our fluency in Swedish to our advantage, especially when people didn't realize how well we understood the language.

Edna farmed, with the help of her son, Dennis, on a place five miles from town. Aunt Hildore's mother also lived in the town, and my recollection of her then is just another old lady with thick stockings peeking out from her long rayon skirts. She always sat primly with her ankles crossed above black oxfords neatly tied with a double knot. Years later I would discover what a kind heart she had when she came to our defense in the face of Hildore's constant nagging in her presence.

After spending a year with Edna, we moved once again when we returned to Dad and Aunt Hildore to live in Edmonton. I don't think I'm exaggerating when I say that marked the beginning of Aunt Hildore's reign of terror. Her earlier conviction that adopting us would disrupt the smooth tenor of her life hardened into active dislike during that time. "I can't do it, I can't do it," we could hear her rail at Dad when we had been shunted down to the basement. And we would hear her cry, "I cannot have those boys living in this house. I hate them!" It is the echo of those words that convinced me it was she who manipulated our future.

Chapter Four
Underground Life

The house Dad found for the family when we moved to Edmonton was dark brown shingle and had been built many years before on 82nd Street. A wooden fence separated it from the house next door, and a hedge bordered the sidewalk like a line dividing it from the world. Striped awnings covered the windows on the upper floor, and the curtains were frequently drawn downstairs as if to conceal the secrets of the family. I always thought the house looked like it was hiding from its neighbors.

Although Linnea and Miriam were allowed to climb the steps to the porch to go into the house by the front door, Duane and I never went in that way. Being a little more cautious by nature, he would grab me by the arm if I suggested we try to sneak in that way and then tug me down the narrow paved walkway that circled round to the kitchen entry. My twin and I suffered many subtle forms of segregation growing up, and to this day I cannot remember one happy day in that house.

It was a pretty simple home and really quite small, only about 1,200 square feet. A faded rag rug covered a small area of the floor in the entrance hall that opened on to the kitchen behind, and the parlor occupied the area to the right. Duane and I only went in there once when a photographer named Mr. Wessel was hired to take a family portrait. Now I think of the picture as propaganda that would prove to the curious that the Vikman household was normal and loving like all the others in the neighborhood. Miriam, wearing a tidy hair ribbon atop her perfectly combed hair, is perched on an overstuffed sofa covered in a drab, green geometric fabric—what today would be described as homely but serviceable—between her parents while Linnea sits aloof from everyone next to a huge radio that they listened to almost as seldom as they used the front room. Except for the design on the sofa, flowers cover every other visible surface and the general effect of the décor is of tired and outmoded Victoriana or what later became known as hand-me-down traditional. Aunt Hildore's only adornment is an oval brooch at the neck of her dark dress, and Dad looks equally stiff in a striped tie similar to a cravat. Duane and I, wearing sweaters and ties, are posed on the floor in front of the couch to complete the family circle. In the style of the photography of the day, no one is smiling, but more than that, no one looks happy, and the general impression is one of moral rectitude.

Behind the parlor there was a dining room, but Duane and I were never allowed to eat in there either. That was only used when there were guests whom Duane and I never joined. From the few quick peeks I took at it, I remember an oval table in need of refinishing and a centerpiece of highly colored improbable looking fruit. A stairway, covered with worn carpeting that might once have been bright red, but had darkened with age to a muddy hue, led to the second floor where there were four rooms including the study. Duane and I didn't share any of them. In fact, we never even saw what they looked like. Nobody actually said, "Don't you dare go into those rooms." We just knew they were forbidden territory.

Our domain lay at the bottom of the basement steps where we were put in the cellar all by ourselves! It was our home—and our prison. The stairs were reached by a door near the stove in the kitchen where drab, brownish linoleum covered the floor. Everything back in that house seems just another shade of dismal. Even today, I can't imagine how much Aunt Hildore must have wished we were living somewhere else because she made sure we were always as far away from her as possible.

The basement was the darkest, most dreary space I have ever had to live in, and Duane and I shared some mighty miserable places when we were boys. The small landing behind the kitchen door was usually cluttered with mops and brooms and an old Bissel carpet sweeper that looked like it might leave as much dirt on the floor as it collected. Antiquated as the equipment looked, however, Aunt Hildore applied it with such vigor that every inch of floor was as sterile as her personality. The stairs themselves were just plain treads with open spaces instead of risers, and I remember being afraid I might fall through when I was first in that house. But even before our eyes had adjusted to the gloom, the dank, musty smell of stagnant air assailed our nostrils. Between that and my fear of plunging into the dark abyss, it took an act of will to continue downwards. At the bottom of the steps, there was just a bare concrete floor made uneven with cracks that had developed over the years. A brave weed occasionally poked through, only to wither away in the darkness. In the center of the room one support pillar carried two water pipes, one each for hot and cold. There was no bathroom, just a toilet that stood in the open space with no enclosure for privacy.

For most of the years that Duane and I lived there, our only furniture was a double bed frame with a skinny mattress—I guess it's a good thing we were pretty thin ourselves. An orange crate was placed on end to hold our wash basin, and our only towel, in reality a faded rag, hung from a nail in the pillar. I guess we were lucky to have that. Over in the corner, the dark abyss of the coal bin yawned below the small opening where the coal was brought into the house. On the opposite wall stood the washtub and an old Maytag washing machine. The only other light came through a tiny window above our cot and another near the washer. If it was a truly bright day out, an occasional shaft of sun would pierce the gloom, but ordinarily there was little difference between morning and night.

If we tried to see if anyone had come into the house, we could occasionally glimpse the shadows of our aunt or uncle's shoes through a glass insulator that was part of an old telephone line. It was attached to a baseboard at the top of the stairs. Sometimes we scrunched down to peer through if we heard the doorbell, but it was impossible to see faces, just legs. Somehow, though, it made us feel a part of the upstairs activities and not so far away. Otherwise, we felt quite alone down there—just two small orphans left to their own devices.

I know that I've tried to forget what it was like to be a captive down there because those memories are just too cruel, but even today I say, "I just can't remember what we thought about all those hours and days down there." Sheer boredom was another obstacle we had to overcome daily. It spread out before us in an unending stream that stretched beyond the horizon of our imaginations. There was nothing to do down there, nothing to see; no place to go. The atmosphere of our basement home was a miasma that assaulted both mind and body.

Perhaps we tried not to think too much because it hurt to know that nobody wanted us around. When I look back, I don't want to recreate in my imagination those two young boys shivering in their hand-me-down, army surplus clothes that were too big when we first wore them and then too small after a few months. Just thinking of it now gives me a creepy, crawly itch. In the ever dim light we frequently felt sleepy as if it was always bedtime and we existed in an eternal night. Fortunately we seldom had nightmares, but we didn't need dark dreams to torment us. The reality was terror enough.

I don't know when my soul started yearning for something beautiful, or when I felt the first fleeting stirrings of optimism. I'm not sure when I began to think in my subconscious about my future and feel a ray of hope. I do know, however, that at some bleak time when I was physically imprisoned down there that some kind of spiritual awakening occurred. From somewhere deep down in my innermost being, in a place that not even Aunt Hildore could breach, came an immense conviction, "If I don't dream now, 'I can make it!' I won't even come close." It was such an indescribable feeling that I couldn't put it into words—I didn't have any idea what "making it" meant and only knew there was a part of me that no one could touch. Perhaps that was where I stored the few kind moments I had enjoyed in life like the memory of Aunt Huldah's gentle reproach when we thought we were helping her and killed the chickens we mistook for crows. I only know that some amorphous belief gave hope to my starved spirit that life could offer greater consolations. I had to hang on to something.

Until our prospects improved when we were fifteen, however, we were imprisoned in that dark place. Our eyes strained to see through the dim light; but what was there to see other than those feet going into the warm kitchen where we were not welcome? Family television was a long way off, and there was no radio for us either.

The doorway to the coal bin held no promise of escape—it was dark and dingy and scary. Who knew what spirits huddled in the corner ready to leap out and grab our legs as we scurried by? Was that where the devil we sometimes heard about in our uncle's sermons lay in wait? Was that coal bin what he meant when he warned about the snares of the devil? On delivery day the coal would thunder down the chute with a terrifying roar that convinced us that demons were charging to get us. Even the pings of the last lumps bouncing in the sudden silence gave us goose bumps until the cheery voice of the driver called, "That's it for the day, Mrs. Vikman."

Sometimes the cellar was a haven, however, particularly when Dad traveled to a conference or meeting out of town. Those absences gave Aunt Hildore even greater opportunity to unleash her anger at the intrusion of the two of us into her carefully regulated home.

Her ears would catch the sound of the kitchen door as we returned from school, and she stood stirring the big pots at the stove. "Dirt," she would scream, stomping her feet, "dirt!" Her arm holding the ladle would rise menacingly in the air as she yelled "dirt" once again at our backs as we tried hurriedly to put the cellar door between us and her frightening figure. Sometimes we weren't quick enough, and with a rough shove, she would push us down the stairs. It's amazing that neither one of us ever broke a bone the way she treated us. She didn't stamp her feet at Miriam or Linnea like that, and I never saw her try to strike either of them.

While I never saw Dad express any physical signs of love towards our aunt, neither did he ever manifest disgust or even disapproval for the way she treated us. I have searched fruitlessly through his papers for old letters or newspaper clippings to discover any information about how they met or where they were married. As a bit of a packrat myself, I find the paucity of his records a telling indication of a lack of sentimentality as well as a hint of his true feelings for her. I now believe that when he married Hildore, he was looking for a woman he thought would make a good minister's wife, a credit to him in the eyes of his congregation, and a caring mother. Perhaps he was trying to hide his disappointment that only some of these hopes held true when he retreated to his study and shut his door, although we always thought he went up there to write for the church bulletin or to prepare his sermons. We were still too young to understand the irony of his exhortations each Sunday to love thy neighbor when his own nephews were on the receiving end of such open dislike. Nevertheless, like blind men who can sense the presence or absence of other people, we guessed when Aunt Hildore had left the house and knew it was safe to creep upstairs to Dad's study. We needed those times to bask, for even a short time, in what we considered the safety of his presence, although in reality he did little to protect us.

Once we dared to call Aunt Hildore "Mom." Her strident response, "I'm not your mother! Your mother's dead! You killed your mother!" stifled any hopes of maternal affection we might have hoped to spark in her heart. We were emotionally starved, hungry for the warm arms that had soothed us as toddlers, but our needs were unfulfilled. Possibly that is why we clung so tenaciously to the idea of Dad's affection and refused, until we were quite mature, to examine his odd behavior. Perhaps, too, we were afraid of losing the small semblance of affection we craved.

On those occasions when we successfully made it up to our uncle's office, the precious time with him lasted only until Aunt Hildore discovered us. She would angrily berate us for sneaking about. Then Dad would just murmur in Swedish, "*Lodem vara, lodem vara,*" (leave them be, leave them be). From the mildness of his tone she would realize that she really hadn't lost her control over him, and he would quickly send us downstairs. Sometimes, when he became aggravated, he would yell those same words, but they had little effect on her in the long run. She knew he would never stay angry with her for long. Why, then, did we never question how tenuous his defense of us was?

After she had discovered us in his study several times, Aunt Hildore had a deadbolt installed on the kitchen side of the basement door which she locked whenever we were in the cellar. The terror of living in the dark became so much worse after that, for we realized our only means of escape had been cut off.

Unwelcoming as the basement was, it usually offered us a safe place. On wash day, however, Aunt Hildore had other opportunities to express her malicious nature. She would march down with a basketful of dirty clothes, looking for all the world like any housewife intent on doing her laundry. But not Aunt Hildore! Grabbing the broom she would try to beat us with it until we cowered under the metal bed. As Duane recently remarked, "She was always mean to us; not one day was she nice to us." He has always been the more outspoken of the two of us.

Coming home from school on cold days, we would frequently find the outer door locked. Even if she was in the kitchen preparing dinner, our aunt would ignore our attempts to open the back door. Sometimes we would try to stay warm just running around, and when that didn't work we would escape from the wind to the summer playhouse. It was only about eight feet by six, but on a bitter winter afternoon it felt like heaven in there. We were never allowed to go into it during vacation, or if the girls wanted to use it, but nobody cared in the wintertime. Otherwise, if luck was with us, we might find the side door of the garage left open, and we could warm ourselves by the gas heater that was always left on. The car had better care than we did in those cold Canadian winters!

Our cellar home was bleak and frequently damp and cold and without each other's company Duane and I would have been destitute. We desperately needed each other. That was never more true than one of the last times we spent Christmas in Edmonton. It was early in the morning as we returned from the midnight service at the church. We were all exhausted and looking forward to bed. As the car turned into the driveway, we were startled by a strange figure jumping from one of the darkened windows of the house. It was too black a night to see the man's features, but I will never forget the sound of his shoes flapping on the driveway.

The poor soul had probably broken into the house to find something to eat and thought no one would be coming home at that hour. We frequently saw jobless men with their haunted, hungry faces downtown. Now, it seemed, one of them had been wandering in our neighborhood and found the seemingly empty house too much of a temptation. It must have been quite a shock for him when he heard our car's engine and the sound of the tires crunching up to the garage.

But it was also a big shock for Dad to discover someone had broken into the house. Looking back, I can't remember if he called the police or if he realized we had returned before the thief had been able to steal anything. I never knew what happened after we went into the house and turned on all the lights to make sure he didn't have an accomplice hiding in one of the closets.

As Duane and I retreated to our hole in the cellar I imagined them all talking excitedly about their terrible experience, and in my mind's eye I saw Aunt Hildore putting a pot of milk on the stove to make cocoa. How I could have thought of that I can't guess because I had never even tasted cocoa—maybe I had read about it in school. What I do know is no one stopped to consider that maybe Duane and I were scared, too. Instead we were just hustled through the kitchen and down the stairs to our makeshift bedroom and left all alone in the dark. Chilled by the apparition that had appeared in the driveway, we felt totally bereft of any bonds of love except for what we could offer each other. We huddled together under our tattered blanket, our bodies locked together as one.

The sound of the deadbolt snapping closed cracked louder than a pistol that night. The finality of the sound was terrifying. If someone else was hiding down there, would anyone know? Would anyone care? Would anyone help us? We clung to each other, our trembling bodies shaking our rickety bed. I don't ever remember being so afraid before or since. Duane's usually protective arms offered little solace that night, and the familiar basement seemed like an alien place. Even the squeak of the bedsprings sent chills through our slight frames.

When we could no longer tolerate the terror of being alone with our fears, we crept to the top of the stairs. We hoped the dim light seeping under the door would offer some consolation. Arms around each other, we spent the rest of the night in sleepless dread amid the mops and brooms. Our panic was more real than the hard step on which we crouched. What ogres visited our sleep in the nights to come we don't remember. Perhaps our minds created a protective shield for memories too harsh for us to understand. If this scenario seems too dramatic even now, I remind myself I was only seven years old that night.

Chapter Five
Outside Faces

We were little moles living underground most of the time, so when we ventured upstairs and out into the world we had to blink to adjust to a different life. We had to pretend we were like other children, no longer the boys oppressed and berated by their angry aunt. We had to put on our outside faces, smiling to mask our sadness or confusion and squaring our shoulders to avert signs of dejection. I was still too young to realize that Dad had an outside face, too.

How Dad permitted the circumstances under which we lived to occur and to continue throughout our childhood is a deep and persistent mystery. Even as a grown man, I still cannot quite fathom his behavior. Young children take love for granted until the opposite proves true, and it seemed to Duane and me, at least in the beginning, that Dad loved us. Now I wonder why we never questioned how different our life was from the one our cousins lived though we were just floors apart.

In the morning, when we joined the family for our usual breakfast of a hot cereal called Sunny Boy, which I still eat today, and eggs that Dad bartered when he preached in the country, Duane and I were never permitted to sit down. There were chairs for Linnea and Miriam and, of course, at the head and foot of the table for our aunt and uncle, but none for us. We stood for virtually every meal. What a picture we would have presented to someone peering through the kitchen window. A stranger would have seen two youngsters shifting from foot to foot, awkwardly trying to butter their toast and keep the crumbs from falling to the floor. Our food was carefully monitored and measured out, and while the girls' glasses were filled to the brim with their milk, we received a diluted mixture, half milk and half water. We filled up on toast.

We came home from school for lunch, and it was almost always the same old bologna sandwiches on white bread and enough water to wash them down. If Aunt Hildore baked any cookies for dessert, she only gave them to Miriam and Linnea; we never got any. We don't know what delicacies she served to company. When a visiting minister or other guests stayed for dinner, we ate first in the kitchen—the only time we had chairs to sit on. When we finished, we were shunted back to our basement quarters.

What kind of a warped spirit could devise such treatment? Did Dad ever protest to Aunt Hildore in private? Was it the need to maintain peace in the household that prevented Dad from intervening in his wife's behavior? Did he fear that if he cracked the fragile calm of his home, it would no longer be possible to present the appearance of a united front to his congregation? Was he afraid of Aunt Hildore? Or did he hesitate to take any steps that might goad her to treat us even more harshly? He had loved his brother, and we thought he loved us, but was it just because of a sense of duty and obligation that he had brought us to Canada? If he had only wanted to prevent us from living in a papist atmosphere at Boys Town in Nebraska, then his failure to act on our behalf might be easy to explain. However, Duane and I fled to the protection of his study whenever we could. Was that to escape the bleakness of the cellar, or did we feel strong blood ties to him despite his failure to protect us from Aunt Hildore? The more I ponder these questions, the more I wonder if we were simply dependent on him and mistook our dependence for love. How did he really feel about us? Why didn't he do more to defend us?

Many years later, Dad told us that Aunt Hildore had suffered a nervous breakdown at some point during the time we spent in Sweden. I didn't know what he meant by that. Knowledge of mental illness was still in its infancy, and any discussion of it was usually hidden behind closed doors. Maybe she suffered from a manic depressive disorder or some other illness for which there was no medication or remedy. There is no record that Dad ever sought any treatment for Aunt Hildore either in Sweden or in Canada.

In the 1930s stress had not yet been clinically defined, and there was still a strong belief that people could control all their behaviors. However, there was no question that Aunt Hildore could treat her own daughters with kindness that she never bestowed on us. Ultimately, all these still beg the question, "Why didn't Dad shelter us from harm?"

If the truth of the conditions at home had been known to the congregation, it would have been difficult for Dad to preach family values and brotherly love convincingly. (In later years we discovered that nothing had been quite as secret as we thought.) Short of committing Aunt Hildore to a mental institution, Dad had to support her in public.

Divorce was an ugly concept in the thirties, and it was the kiss of death for a minister who wanted to keep his church. In fact, the word divorce shocked and embarrassed most people. In many places divorce was assumed to involve sexual misconduct. There was less concern about living within a fractured, dysfunctional family and more concern about what other people would think if the family fell apart.

It's possible that Dad felt trapped between our needs and those of his wife and that he took the coward's way out by simply avoiding the issue. He couldn't take any chances of the church ladies gossiping over their grocery baskets and exclaiming, "Did you know that the Vikman boys don't even have a chair to sit on?" or "Someone said that Duane and Edwin sleep in the basement!" That kind of chatter would have doomed Dad's popularity in the community and the Lutheran ministry. The people in our world lived by a "practice what you preach" rule, making it impossible for Dad to separate from Aunt Hildore and still maintain his job and status as pastor.

Dad didn't earn much money, but in the years of the Depression any salary was valued. Even more important at that time was the respect that the pastor held, occupying a position that a divorce would have shattered. Speculative as all these questions may be, the undisputable fact is that we, the two little moles, lived a double life between the cellar at 10924 82nd Street and the world at large.

Sometimes Miriam had friends over after school. The girls would tromp in the front door and through the hallway into the kitchen for something to eat. Aunt Hildore never yelled at them to clean off their feet. Before we were chased to the cellar, we would get a glimpse of tall glasses of lemonade or milk and see the plate of cookies set out on the table for their snack. Sitting in the dark on our bed, our stomachs would rumble as we thought of the food being devoured upstairs and of how long we would have to wait until our dinner. We had treats so seldom that we weren't quite sure what we were missing.

In warm weather, our cousins and their friends spent most of the time in the playhouse. If it was cold or rainy, I think they played in the girls' bedrooms. On those days, before they got out their puzzles or their new Monopoly game, they sat at the scarred wooden table in the kitchen. Linnea, in particular, would make smacking noises as she devoured the goodies that she never shared. It seemed as if she wanted to emphasize that she had something we didn't. But Linnea just pointed to the door to the cellar, and we would disappear.

"Wouldn't you think," Duane or I might ask the other when we were alone, "that a girl who is so stuck up would be more careful about the way she eats?"

I don't know if the friends who came were ever curious about where we slept. Maybe they assumed there were comfortable rooms in the basement. Maybe, like most children, they never really gave it much consideration. I've often thought how strange it was that they never noticed there weren't any toys around for us.

I remember two girls—Shirley Dean, whom we got to know in later years, and her friend Nora Moffat, who lived only a few houses down the block—often came over. After a while, since their families didn't belong to a church, they started coming to ours and eventually became confirmed there. That makes it even stranger that they exhibited so little curiosity about us. Maybe they were discouraged if they did.

Another measure of our insignificance sailed completely over my head, although now I can't figure out why. Every once in a while someone we met, probably at church, would notice us to the extent that they would exclaim, "My, you've grown since the last time we saw you." I never gave such comments any thought, and strange as it may seem, we never cared about how old we were. We couldn't escape knowing we were twins because people frequently confused us with one another and then remarked how much we looked alike, but we never celebrated our birthdays. Bizarre as it may seem, we didn't think about them either, but that is undoubtedly testament to how little we knew about social conventions and how successfully Aunt Hildore brain-washed us. I assume that Miriam and Linnea blew out candles on their cakes every year, but if so we were sent from the table before they did. If we ever received party invitations from one of our classmates we never heard about them. I know we never went to such parties and would not have had any presents to bring anyway.

Keeping up appearances played a big part in our lives. No matter how bad things were at home, we never spoke about it to the neighbors. I don't remember being told not to say anything, but it was another intuitive understanding of our circumstances.

After school we ran around the neighborhood with the guys who lived near us, and sometimes on a rainy day we played at their houses. Those were pretty special occasions.

At first Duane and I weren't sure how to react when we were invited. I remember how our friends would run into their kitchens calling, "Mom, we're home! We're starved!" More often they would be greeted with a hug and a kiss, and there would be a welcoming smile for us. "How would you like a glass of milk?" we would be asked. Maybe we'd be greeted with the aroma of cookies just out of the oven or a bowl of apples with shiny red and green cheeks. That was pure heaven.

The boys' rooms were full of toys that they had gotten for Christmas or birthdays. Even in the days leading up to World War II, when memories of the Depression were still raw, they might have a new toy car or game. The best times were when we played with someone who recognized that Duane and I never brought anything from our own house, and they would offer to loan us a toy.

We became adept at recognizing which toys we could copy for ourselves, but finding the right materials to construct a car, for example, proved to be a formidable obstacle. When we confided this problem to our friend Kazmeer, he told us about the box factory where his father, a contractor, bought his lumber. It was a short walk for us, down the trash filled alley behind our house, where we could collect discarded wood scraps to carve. It was pretty simple for us to whittle the pieces into shapes resembling our old Chevy, and we made wheels from empty spools that our aunt had thrown away after a sewing project. We could usually find some discarded paint to add the finishing touches.

I recall one other occasion when Hildore was outfoxed and completely nonplussed by a dinner invitation Duane and I received from a family at church. Einar Carlson had also emigrated from Sweden, and he must have enjoyed the opportunity to talk to us in his own language. Hildore apparently couldn't devise a legitimate reason to refuse, so she let us go. Shortly thereafter, Einar's two sisters, who owned the apartment building they all lived in, came to our house for dinner, but we, of course, weren't included. They spied us as we were leaving the kitchen, and calling out to us, they gave us each a dime. That night we ran around the corner to the nearest grocery store, and we each bought a bag of candy. The Carlson sisters might have been the first to recognize how our lives differed from the rest of the family.

I'm afraid we were equally resourceful in perpetuating the pretense that everything was normal in our house on 82nd Street, particularly on Sundays.

Each weekend, dressed up in pants and shirts—the nearest outfits we ever had to suits like the other boys wore—and squeaky clean from the Saturday night baths—except for mealtimes the only time we were allowed upstairs— we attended church with the family.

Those Sundays provided another opportunity for us to spend a little time alone with Dad. We could sit quietly with him while he polished his sermon and got ready for the service, and we found those moments to be a time of great solace. If our aunt caught us in his church office, she could only give us a dirty look, since she had to take care that no parishioners saw her behaving badly. Her hands were tied in those moments. She couldn't send us home, and she certainly couldn't stamp her foot and call us dirt, or awful boys, or any other names.

But Dad also acted as if those times with him were everyday occurrences and not rare instances of togetherness. In those moments, everyone wore their outside faces. We exuded sweetness and light, love and devotion, and now, I realize, everyone wore a mask.

Shortly after our sixth birthday, Dad started sending us to live with the first of eleven different foster families. This would be our existence until we were fifteen. These were usually short-term arrangements, and we would return to Edmonton and the cellar when we were no longer wanted or needed by those families. It was hard for us to understand why we were shunted from place to place, but now I realize it was mostly to fill in during emergencies— the sudden illness of other workers or a family death—but it is still difficult to comprehend considering our age. Most of the people were also glad to get the cash that he gave them from what he called the Orphans' Fund— money that I think he got from the Lutheran Church to subsidize our upbringing. The source of this has never been quite clear to us, since it is a fact that he never formally adopted Duane and me, and no government social services existed in either Canada or the United States at that time.

Most of these families considered us to be hired help, but a few of them treated us with dignity, and even when they expected us to work hard and pitch in with all the farm or house work, they were kind to us. We were never spoiled, but some people, like the Tennis and Johansen families, regarded us as they would their own children. Sometimes these families gave us our own room; and sometimes we shared with their children, but we always had plenty to eat and enough milk to drink. Men, like Fritz Johansen, might scold when we misbehaved or seemed lazy in performing our chores, but they never beat us or punished in other physical ways. One of the best memories I have is staying with Adeline Tennis during a summer when Dad took his family to the tiny cabin he owned at Seba Beach.

Adeline was a pretty girl—or did I just think so because she treated us with compassion and understood the special needs we had as orphans? She lived with her parents in a big house in the country near Meeting Creek. The yard was surrounded by a white picket fence, and every night we ate vegetables from the large garden by the kitchen door. The house looked very grand to us—it was by far the nicest home we had ever seen and would be the finest one we would live in until we could buy our own many years later. I remember asking Duane, "Do you think heaven will be as pretty as this?" I'm surprised I didn't equate our cellar with heaven's opposite.

Adeline taught us to ride the family's horse, which was a skill we would use over and over in the years to come. Though she was several years older—probably about seventeen—she always planned activities for us. At night, we would all gather round the kitchen table to play board games or listen to the radio. I remember laughter at funny stories and affectionate teasing when someone made a silly mistake. Nothing so good-natured ever happened in Edmonton. At long last we were part of a family.

Occasionally, we would careen around the fields with playmates wielding pretend pistols and wearing old bandanas over our faces, playing cowboys and Indians. These were pleasant interludes for us, a few bright spots in an otherwise bleak existence, and they made good memories. Mostly, however, our foster parents were hardened, pessimistic people who had been disillusioned by the rampant joblessness and poverty of the era, and they viewed us as cheap help. As a result, we never knew that childhood was supposed to be a joyful time of life.

We had a seesaw existence—some ups, but more downs, and the occasional sudden drop. We always struggled to be at the top. It was the memories of the decent families that fueled the dreams I needed in order to look beyond the present. I don't think I could have survived without the certainty of a brighter future, and my usually optimistic spirit was an important support for Duane's more dour nature.

Much as we hated the Edmonton cellar, it had at least become familiar to us. As we began to move from place to place, the lack of stability, combined with not knowing where we would be sleeping next, was completely unnerving. We never knew when Dad would announce a new departure—destination unknown. Occasionally, we would have some idea that we were leaving a few days before; at other times, Dad would just announce, "Boys, it's time to go." We would hurriedly throw our few belongings into our satchel and follow him out to the car. It might be four-thirty or five o'clock in the morning.

If we were going too far for Dad to drive us—or if it was inconvenient—we would arrive early at the train station. It was often windy and bitingly cold in winter and suffocating in summer as we waited on the platform, but the temperature didn't really make much difference. We wore pretty much the same pants and lightweight jackets with zippers throughout the seasons. We just didn't bother with our caps in July and August.

We almost never knew where we were going and often didn't even know the names of our next family. Our destination didn't matter, since we had little sense of the geography of the vast plains surrounding Edmonton. Names of people and places were far less important than how we were treated.

Today, Duane and I look back and see two small boys waiting patiently for the next ride to who knew where, both literally and figuratively. The train would chug into sight, its massive engine towering above us and often belching a black snort of smoke as the engineer sounded the whistle to announce its arrival. We would strain to haul ourselves up the steep metal steps, dragging our suitcase behind us and watch as Dad handed a note to the conductor, instructing him where to let us off. "The family will be there to meet you," he would mutter to us before he swung around and back onto the platform.

Duane and I pressed our noses against the windows to catch a last glimpse of Dad. We could see his lips moving and ours would respond as we whispered our "good-byes." He would stand waving, then start to run down the platform as the train picked up speed. He'd try to match it, increasing his pace until he could no longer keep up, and as he started to disappear from our view, he'd lift his arm in a last farewell salute. With that he would be gone. Duane and I so needed love that I wonder now if we interpreted Dad's show of affection correctly. If he was sorry to see us leave, why was he sending us away? If he didn't care, was all this just posturing for others to admire?

We would be left all alone to meet total strangers. The tracks would lead us to face our new employers, who could be called that only in the sense that we would work for them, not that we would be paid. Actually, with the money Dad sent them, they were by and large the ones who profited, but we didn't know that back then.

It wasn't until the probability of a longer-term stay in Fort Saskatchewan arose when we were seven years old that Dad tried to explain why we would be leaving once again. Duane and I wouldn't be living in Edmonton again for many months, he said, maybe more than a year. We were too young to understand the possible ramifications of this longer absence. It seems incomprehensible now that Dad didn't seem to consider the dangers of sending children to people he barely knew, if he knew them at all. It obviously never occurred to him to probe very deeply into why perfect strangers would want to take two little boys into their homes unless it were for motivations of money—or worse. No background or character checks occurred, nor were there social service agencies to supervise our care.

I will always remember the July night in 1938 when Dad called us into the study. There was a peculiar look on his face as he motioned us to sit down. He ran his hands through his hair as if he was putting off what he had to say. "Boys," he finally began, a strange tone in his voice, not one we were used to hearing. "Boys," he said again. "Mom and I have been talking, and we've thought long and hard about what I'm going to tell you. It's important you listen carefully, since I want you to understand everything. You need to know why you go to live other places sometimes." Even now I'm not sure he appreciated the fact that we were really too young to understand this odd circumstance. "Now," he continued, "you've probably overheard people talking, and you know life is hard for some folks around here. I'm sure you've heard them speak about the Depression. For many people that means no jobs, so they don't have much money, even some who used to be rich. Well, Mom and I have decided that you boys could go live with some of them for a longer time, and with the money we could give them from your orphans' fund, they would be able to buy food for their families. Isn't that a wonderful way to help? Mom was sure you'd think so." (It was always an enigma to me that Dad insisted on referring to her as Mom although she had vehemently refused to let us call her that when we had first come to live with them.)

I've always believed it was really Aunt Hildore who conceived this plan and that she hoped to convince Dad it would be a good way to assist other people in that bad economy. I can just hear her saying, "Now, Arvid, you know the boys would be happy to help out." She probably persuaded him with a further argument, "Living in the country would be so healthy for them." I wonder if he really bought this line of reasoning, but I don't believe she was motivated at all by a generosity of spirit. I think she seized upon a ruse that she expected to appeal to Dad's better instincts as well as to test what she recognized as an inherent weakness in his character. He would almost certainly cave in to almost any whim of hers—even if he disagreed with its legitimacy.

It has been too many years since this conversation with Dad occurred to assess his motivations in a totally satisfactory way—the fact stands that he consented to send us away. Aunt Hildore had cleverly concocted a way to rid herself of two very annoying nephews without seeming to be a bit selfish.

Naturally, we did not understand then that Dad existed in a state of denial about her true nature. In retrospect, I think he was more of a yes-man than his congregation guessed, at least as far as his wife was concerned. It was just easier to follow the path of least resistance and fall in with her plans.

Charles Berdahl, a former Lutheran minister and one of the two men to whom this book is dedicated, has suggested that Dad could have been the kind of cleric who didn't pay much attention to everyday life because he was married to the church and would give all his energy to being the pastor. His wife would be left in charge of the family and all things domestic. Added to this could have been Dad's firm conviction that Jesus had given him the call to "go and do the work," and he was therefore released from the more mundane matters of the world. I now believe that Dad's adherence to the teachings of the popular nineteenth century revivalist preacher, C. O. Rosenius (1816-68) may have become so extreme that he had become one of those men for whom the activities of daily Christian living became subservient to hollow declarations of dogma. I knew that he, like almost every Swedish male who arrived in this country, had packed his family Bible, his psalm book, and his *postilla* (collections of Rosenius sermons) to use for daily devotions. For the most part, these religious practices fostered strong family ties, but in rare cases where the letter of the law, rather than the spirit, prevailed, piety became hypocrisy and evolved into pietism. I am afraid Dad had become a pietist.

Duane and I had adjusted somewhat to the shorter visits to strangers, but we were utterly bewildered by this new concept of being away for months at a time, and we barely heard Dad's further explanations that this would never be a permanent situation. I have a vague recollection of his voice assuring us that we would always have a home in Edmonton, and that "Mom and I will always be here if you need us." I wonder now if he was trying to convince himself as much as us that this plan could possibly bode well for our future. It might have been one of the last times that he recognized what pawns he had allowed us to become, and he was suffering some last minute misgivings. But even as he continued to talk as if this was all Mom's idea and something he wasn't totally buying into, I remember him adding, "But Mom has suggested you'd have fun living with new people. She called it an adventure." At a much later time I recalled that Dad never once said, "I think it's a wonderful opportunity for you."

All of a sudden, this plan wasn't sounding good to me at all. Mom never wasted any time on us, and if she thought of us at all, it meant she was probably devising some new punishment or mean trick. I was far too young to have developed a cynical streak, but I certainly felt uneasy. I had never heard the term 'fear of the unknown' but that is what I was feeling. What was going to happen to Duane and me? "Now with this new plan," Dad continued, "you'd be doing a good deed, and it would give you a chance to live away from the city, too."

Later, when members of the church or neighbors would exclaim, "Why, where have you boys been?" or "we haven't seen you in the longest time, don't you miss it here in Edmonton?" we would usually answer, "we would really rather live on the farm than in the city." We didn't realize we were unconsciously echoing Dad. I imagine our aunt smiled inwardly whenever she heard that, but I'm not sure we fooled all the curious.

"Of course," Dad went on, "you'll be expected to do some of the chores, maybe even learn something about how to plant seed, or plow, or even milk the cows when you're on a farm. Sometimes, you may be living with people in the country who don't have electricity like we have here, and you'll be taught how to pump water and how to use a kerosene lamp. Just think, it'll be like living in the old days like when you play frontier! I promise you, though, you'll always get to go to school." I poked Duane in the ribs at that. Maybe our new life wouldn't be too bad, but I would have felt fine if he'd left out the school part.

"Do you think any of the people will have sons we can play with?" I asked with anticipation. "I hope they don't just have girls."

Our experience with the opposite sex by then was limited to our sisters, whom we hardly remembered, and to Miriam and Linnea, who ignored us most of the time. Of course, that was better than the mean looks they threw our way, especially Linnea, who seemed to take a perverse pleasure in the way her mother treated us. In fact, Linnea's behavior frequently mirrored Aunt Hildore's. She delighted in playing nasty jokes on us, like locking us out of the playhouse on cold days when she knew it was the only place we could get warm. "Oh," she'd laugh when we got into the kitchen at the end of the afternoon. "You look so funny with your lips so blue!"

"Well, I don't know about girls—we won't really know until you get to each home," Dad's voice brought us back. "You'll just have to wait and see.

I know they won't have much money. They'll be happy when they can use yours. Now, off to bed, boys, because tomorrow you're meeting your new family, and we have to get an early start in the morning."

We were accustomed to obeying and not questioning our uncle's plans, so that night we packed our meager belongings in the little suitcase we used whenever we went someplace over night. It had a worn leather handle and brass locks that stuck when we tried to open them. I think it might even have been the one we used going to Aunt Huldah's when we were babies, since I once found a tag for the Swedish American line caught in the torn lining. We stored the bag in the basement when it wasn't being used, so it had a horrid, musty smell. Our clothes probably had the same odor, but we didn't notice it most of the time.

Duane and I had lived in so many different places in the United States, Sweden and Canada that we were adjusting to our vagabond existence. Normally, we didn't feel exactly excited or scared when another move seemed imminent, nor did we wonder to one another what might lie in store for us. We didn't question Dad. We accepted life as it happened, not comprehending its bizarre twists.

This time, however, something sounded different to me. Maybe it was the tone of Dad's voice as he knelt down with us to lead us in our nightly prayers. Perhaps it was doubt I heard creeping into his voice or the recognition of his own hypocrisy in conducting this evening ritual. We intoned the familiar "Now I lay me down to sleep, I pray the Lord my soul to keep." Dad never missed a night, and we weren't old enough to question why he didn't do some of the "keeping" himself, but instead kept sending us away.

"I'm a little worried," I muttered to myself, "it sounds like we might be gone an awfully long time." Fortunately, as we settled to sleep in our solitary cave that night, neither Duane nor I could truly guess how good our meager quarters would begin to look in the months ahead. Our life journey was about to take its ugliest turn yet.

Chapter Six
The Executioner

The name of the family we were sent to was Grandahl, and from the moment we arrived, I knew it wasn't going to be a good time for us. Our new home seemed ordinary enough—there were two stories—but again our living conditions were a bit unusual. In addition to the father, Ted, and the mother, whose name I have forgotten, there were six daughters—Jeanette, Doris, Gladys, Helen, Ruth and Irene—who ranged in age from six to about twenty. The family already filled the four upstairs rooms, and there wasn't any basement or attic or other space for us to sleep. The Grandahl's had rigged a makeshift bedroom for us in the dining room. Ted had fastened eyehooks on the walls and strung a bedsheet on a clothesline across the room to create a place for the one single bed and dresser they had available.

What a strange life we were having. We had felt so alone in the cellar in Edmonton, and now we could never get away from everyone. We hadn't shared such small quarters with so many people before, and whatever we had thought we knew about girls, we were soon going to learn more. "Oh, Duane," I confided, "we don't have any privacy—they'll be able to hear everything we say."

The first time we wanted a drink of water, we discovered that the Grandahl home in Fort Saskatchewan had no indoor plumbing. Since there was no running water in the house, we had to go outside to get it from the well. Worse yet, we had to adjust to using an outhouse, and that ugly structure was almost as dark as the coal bin at Dad's. "Ooh," I whined when we first went outside, "watch out for the cobwebs and the spiders. They're all over! I hope the bugs don't bite us!"

I didn't yet know how much we would learn to hate living at the Grandahls, for there were many unpleasant surprises to come. One of the first shocks was discovering that there were no partitions between the three commodes in the outhouse, and the girls were so used to using them that they didn't expect to have any privacy or to offer it to anyone else. After a while, Duane and I learned to ignore their presence whenever we had to use the facility. He was accomplished at pretending a problem didn't exist if he had absolutely no control over it.

We had barely been in the house for an hour when Mr. Grandahl began barking out his demands and listing our responsibilities. It was clear from the start that his expectations were a lot bigger than we were. For example, Duane and I divided the chore of bringing in the water used each day for cooking and washing with the oldest girls, but there wasn't even a pump out in the yard. All the water had to be drawn from a well. Now, there is something about a well, with its wooden bucket, that people like to romanticize, but cranking it up was a huge task for my seven-year-old arms. When that job was done, the pail still had to be carried into the house. If too much water spilled, it just meant going through the whole operation all over again.

It took three or four buckets to fill the reservoir by the side of the stove where the water stayed warm for washing clothes and dishes, and then we had to fill another bucket next to the kitchen door for the drinking water. There was always a dipper there if anyone got thirsty. It didn't take much aggravation to stoke Mr. Grandahl's anger, and it flared to a dangerous degree if he found the drinking bucket dry. I discovered this painfully one day.

Unfortunately, I was the only one in the house that afternoon when Mr. Grandahl came in, hot and sweaty from his work at the prison. He had cut across the field and looked forward to a dipper of water to quench his thirst. "What," he roared, "no water for a man when he's put in a long day's work?"

Poor me! I was the only one in sight. I cringed as the big man lunged at me, ducking and backing into a corner, for he was much bigger and quicker than I. "But, but," I stammered as I escaped through the kitchen door, "it's not my turn to fill it today."

I never made that mistake again, and I learned a quick lesson. His great fist caught me on the cheek and slammed into my head, knocking me to the ground. Then he straddled my prone body, and holding his legs over mine so that I couldn't move, he slapped me, and slapped me, and slapped me again until I lost consciousness.

Lucky for me, my good friend Johnny—Duane and I called him JAM from his initials for Johnny Allen Martin—came around the corner just then to see if I could play. He quickly ran home crying, "Mommy, Mommy, Ed's just lying on the ground, not moving. You gotta come quickly!"

But when Mrs. Martin got there, Mr. Grandahl just shook his head and muttered, "Oh, he just fell off the roof. I told him not to go up there."

Since it was only about nineteen miles from Edmonton to Fort Saskatchewan, Dad made Aunt Hildore go to me when he heard the story—maybe Mrs. Martin called him. But my aunt apparently believed what Mr. Grandahl said and just went back to her house in Edmonton. Who would believe a little boy's word against a grown-up's, especially if he was being disobedient? Everybody around the countryside knew that Grandahl had a really mean streak, but most of them were afraid of him, too. After all, he worked at the prison. Who would want to argue with him?

We played with JAM whenever there was time after we'd finished our chores, and we really liked him, but he was unwittingly responsible for one painful attack of jealously that sticks out in my mind.

"Go higher, go higher," we would urge each other as we took turns on the swing set near his house. Legs pumping furiously, we would soar skyward. One afternoon JAM lost his grip and tumbled to the hard ground where the grass was worn away from the scraping of our feet. At first, he just lay there slightly stunned, and then his loud screeches brought his mother running frantically out her kitchen door. Duane and I watched with amazement as she hugged and kissed him and said, "You come home with Mommy, and she'll make you cookies and make you all better."

She never realized that as the swing had continued its arc, it had hit Duane in the head, too, and the tears were spilling down his cheeks as well. I didn't know then what envy felt like, but I knew no one had ever consoled us like that—and I wanted that very badly.

We were still at the Grandahls in 1938 when we sensed an air of anticipation and excitement and we soon heard the girls chattering about the exposition that took place every summer. They talked about exhibits and amusement rides, and it was clear that this would be a welcome break in their usually humdrum lives. Mrs. Grandahl overheard Duane and me speculating about what it would be like and was quick to interject, "Sorry, boys, you can't go with us." To temper our disappointment she added, "But we'll have a bang-up party when it's over." That never happened, but we also found out that the fair was just something for her daughters to talk about. The Grandahls were too cheap to pay the entry fees, and the girls were all just spectators, looking on from the outside.

I remember another time when we had a real problem at that place. The girls in the family had inherited a mean streak from their father, especially Irene, the oldest. Since it was really hard work to get water into the house, we took turns having baths, and we didn't get them often. There wasn't a real bathroom since there was no running water, and they just dragged the washtub into a small closet.

It just so happened that Duane's bath day came on a Saturday night when Irene had a date. She was anxious to primp and get ready, and we felt sure she would preempt his turn. We were quite surprised, then, to hear her call, "Duane, Duane, I've fixed your water. Hurry up and take your bath. I want to take one, too!"

"Why is she being so nice?" I wondered, but I thought it was because she was so pleased this boy was coming to take her out. She'd been talking about him for days. "Oooh," she would squeal, "he's got the cutest dimple," or "he walked on line with me," or something we boys thought sounded equally dumb. Duane surely should have suspected something when she was letting him take a bath before the hot water was used up. "She was just like her daddy," I told a friend when I was many years older. "She didn't have a nice bone in her body,"

Poor Duane. It was usually so dim in the closet that it was hard to see. He got out of his clothes, grabbing his towel as he ran, and jumped into the tub. His screams rang through the little house as scalding water splashed all over his bare legs. The water was so hot he couldn't even move at first; he was paralyzed with the combination of surprise and searing pain.

I don't remember if he got out himself or if Mrs. Grandahl pulled him from the water. All I know is he cowered, gasping with fright and the pain of it all, and everyone just stood there, staring—all except Irene, who covered her face with her hands. I didn't know if she was laughing, or crying, or scared that maybe this time she had gone too far.

At first, Duane's skin turned an ugly bright red, but blisters soon appeared, so Mrs. Grandahl applied the only first aid she knew. She liberally slathered lard all over his second degree burns; no one knew then that applying cool water would reduce the swelling and wrapping loose bandages might prevent infection. Nothing would have been antiseptic anyway, so short of going to a doctor, her antidote was fairly effective.

The pain kept Duane awake most of the night, and when he did sleep, he thrashed around trying to find a comfortable position. It's a wonder the whole family wasn't up all night, too, the way those springs creaked. I know I was.

At times like this Duane showed a streak of stoicism—he refused to cry and all I could do was put my arms around him and ask, "Are you going to be all right?" The answer was usually a laconic, "I'll be okay."

We never asked Irene if she had a good time on her date that evening.

I think someone must have called Dad after this incident, but he was probably busy at one of the churches because the next morning Aunt Hildore arrived. By then pustules were spreading all over Duane's legs. "Maybe she's come to take us home," we hoped.

It's hard to believe, but at that point even her cellar seemed pretty good to us. But of course we should have known better about Aunt Hildore, too. After looking Duane over and having a piece of Mrs. Grandahl's Swedish rye bread and butter, she declared, just like the time she had come after Mr. Grandahl knocked me out, "He'll be all right—they're just complainers." Then back she drove to Edmonton. However, Dad's conscience might have pricked him a bit about this latest episode, for he returned about six weeks later to bring us home with him. I've often wondered what Aunt Hildore told him to make him wait so long.

"Did you know," I asked Duane a few years later, "that old Mr. Grandahl was the executioner at the Fort Saskatchewan prison?" "Of course," he responded, "he sure tried to kill us more than once."

Chapter Seven
Heartbreak

Another particularly harsh memory lingers from the day we earned our first dollar, a veritable fortune in 1940 and a sum which would now have the buying power of about sixteen dollars. That winter, we were living with the Larson family down by the river in the Varscona section of Edmonton— about two miles from our house. We stayed with them intermittingly whenever they needed the kind of cheap labor we provided, and we could easily walk to school when we lived with them.

I remember that Ellen, the wife, acted fairly toward us, but her husband was vindictive. She rarely spoke when he was around the house, and I think he bullied her as much as he did us. Ellen had long hair that she wore in a braid wound around her head, and she would nervously twist the stray curls that hung over her forehead when he yelled at her. As if she knew she'd be punished for showing us any favoritism, she was careful to hide the cookies she planned to give us as an after school treat if he came home unexpectedly. Gus became angry if we didn't obey him or complete our work to his satisfaction. He would beat us with the buckle on the end of his belt until it hurt so much we cried. It's amazing how petty and nasty some people can be, and how they can find happiness being cruel to others. Gus was that kind of man. Duane and I used to nurse our injuries and vowed that we would never treat anyone like this; we promised to defend anyone we saw being beaten when we got bigger. Until that time came, however, we seized any opportunity we could to stay out of his way on the rare days we had a free afternoon.

When this happened, we would try to find odd jobs to earn the spare change Dad told us we needed if we wanted to buy something for ourselves. About the last time we were with the Larsons, when we were barely nine years old, we started a job delivering pamphlets for Premier Advertising

Distributing, a local Edmonton firm. Dad had found a notice of this in the *Edmonton Journal* and suggested we apply. Two mysteries remain—how two forlorn waifs succeeded in being selected, when many older boys or men must have answered the ad, or even more important, how we kept Gus from finding out about the money we earned. We were paid the princely sum of ten cents per hundred pamphlets delivered, and we were proud of our earning power.

The sun had usually hidden behind iron gray clouds and the short winter days had turned bitterly cold when we set out after school about three-thirty each afternoon. Fortunately, the tiny homes—they were only about 1,000 square feet in Varscona—had been built close together, so Duane and I could move quickly up the straight concrete walks as we slogged from door to door in the icy winds, slipping the flyers under door mats or in the cracks between the doors and the sills. The houses were finished with stucco made at a local cement factory and were sprayed with a dull cream paint that had turned grimy over the years. The little adornment they had were lackluster brown or black shutters that seemed especially stark in the waning light.

We took the brochures to school and stored them in our lockers so we could make the most of the few daylight hours as we marched up and down opposite sides of the street. We did this for about a week, and when we had completed our rounds in that neighborhood, we trudged up a nearby hill past a large soccer field to bigger houses that were a little more upscale with larger lots and gardens. The surroundings weren't quite as washed out as those near Larson's, but the winds seemed even stronger up there, and it took longer to get from door to door.

On our last day, we got so cold we even made a bonfire from some of the pamphlets to keep warm. We had delivered to all the houses within walking distance and felt somewhat disheartened when we returned to the company office near the imposing Macdonald Hotel to turn in the last of the pamphlets. To our great glee, the manager counted the remaining leaflets and paid us for all the rest— including those that had gone up in smoke! In our innate honesty, we had even admitted to using some of his flyers as hand-warmers. What we did next with our earnings astonishes me even after over seventy years!

Exiting the office onto Jasper Avenue lined with its two or three storied brick offices and stores, we hurried with our newly earned money past the Piggly Wiggly and the drugstore. As we headed to the five-and-ten-cent store, we hardly noticed the barber shop with its revolving red and white pole or the Army Navy store where Aunt Hildore bought our clothes. In those days you could buy almost anything at the dime store from pots and pans, to undershirts and socks, to notebooks and pencils. There was a soda fountain where shoppers bought soft drinks or sandwiches, but Duane and I liked the toy aisle best. We would gape at the latest model cars and trucks, the brightly painted tops, the jump ropes and hard rubber balls; we would imagine what we could draw with the colorful arrays of chalk, crayons, and paints, and we admired the brightly illustrated books even though we could hardly read them. Most of these cost twenty-five cents or less, and what a treasure trove our dollar could have bought.

Sometimes, we would wander into the stores just to get warm, but that afternoon we had money in our pockets and sped straight for the small Delft doll we had spied in the shop window a few days earlier. Duane and I had stood in awe just gazing at her. "I think it's the most beautiful doll in the world," I had breathed in a whisper. "I want to buy it for Aunt Hildore."

I have no idea why I had thought of that or why my brother agreed, but now we had the money. What could have prompted me to think of this? Did I hope it might spark a little love for us in her heart? Was life at the Larsons so much worse than sleeping in our cellar that I wanted to go home and hoped a gift would soften our aunt's heart? I can't begin to guess what could have given me a glimmer of hope that she would look on us with even a hint of favor.

That must have been the first time I felt the impulse to do something for another individual with little certainty the gesture would be returned. Whatever the motive, we proudly approached the clerk at the cash register to make our purchase, and I remember that in our excitement we spilled all the coins on the worn linoleum as we emptied our pockets.

"Look, over there, Duane," I pointed out as I spied a nickel under one counter. He dove for that one while I spotted several pennies under another. Then we had to count it all out while the grown-ups behind us smiled indulgently at our enthusiasm and waited patiently as we completed our purchase. Finally, we paid for the doll and watched as the saleswoman carefully wrapped it in brown paper and tied the string in a double knot. Oh, we were excited!

"Hurry, hurry," I rushed my brother as we raced down the street toward home. We dashed up the stairs at the front of the house, somehow managing to unwrap the package as we moved. We were so sure Aunt Hildore would love this doll just as much as we did. In our innocence we must have hoped this tiny gift would change our lives. We ran across the porch and rang the doorbell. I'm amazed now at our audacity because Aunt Hildore would never have answered if she'd known it was us. She must have thought someone else was coming to call, because she had removed her apron when she opened the door.

We called excitedly, "Aunt Hildore, Aunt Hildore!"

I will never ever forget what happened next if I live to be a hundred, and I'm pretty close to that now. Aunt Hildore took one look at us, and then at the doll. "Scram," she yelled, "beat it!" And seizing the doll we so gladly thrust out to her, she threw it on the floor and smashed it to pieces. Only our hearts were more shattered.

If we ever entertained the idea of running away from our aunt and uncle, that incident would have been the moment, but we never gave it a thought. First of all, I guess we had no place to go. Second, using today's idiom, we were programmed to obey. We just went where we were told, and when Aunt Hildore told us to scram, we scurried back to the Larson's, our eyes filled with unspilled tears. We were too dispirited to talk about this episode for many years. Even today, when I ponder this question of escape, I can only conclude that this was the only life we knew and Dad and Mom and Linnea and Miriam were all the family we had. A strange bond connected us, and although I can't quite say we were brainwashed, we were certainly conditioned to accept life as we knew it.

Chapter Eight
School Daze

During the time we lived in Canada we had no one to share confidences with, and as we settled in bed for the night, we had little optimism that things might look better in the morning. Daybreak brought scant relief on most days. Our aunt's scowl would greet us instead of the gentle good morning she used for her daughters. We were cramped and tired from sleeping in the basement, and the morning porridge was small comfort. It had usually gotten cold by the time we were allowed to eat, and the prospect of another day at school wasn't a happy thought either.

Walking to school, however, was the one time we could enjoy Miriam's company without Linnea, since it didn't seem to bother her to be seen with us— her friends, Nora and Shirley, didn't mind being with us either. Leaving by the kitchen door, we just had to walk a short block down 82nd Street to Nora's and just a little farther to pick up Shirley. The houses here were bigger than the ones down by Larson's, but still smaller than those nearer the center of Edmonton by the hotel, and some, like ours, were frame rather than stucco. Kicking at the fallen leaves or oddments of debris that littered the alley ways, we would join in the girls' laughter even when we had no idea what their jokes meant. We savored these moments when we could pretend that our hearts were light and carefree.

By the time we reached our classroom doors, however, the sight of the black board and desks reminded us of the reality of our situation. Reading and writing always presented a problem, since we never spoke English consistently before we were eight or nine years old. We had spoken Swedish while we lived with Aunt Huldah and Dad, and Aunt Hildore frequently reverted to their first language at home. When we first started school, we only attended sporadically because we moved so frequently. The hard truth was that we had barely learned to read or write by the time we were ten. No wonder we hated school.

When we were given a vocabulary list to study, we hardly knew where to start. One word might begin with *l* and then the next with *o*, and we didn't even know the alphabet, much less the order the letters came in. It's impossible to find a word in the dictionary if you don't know that *m* comes before *n*. Besides that, we rarely had access to a dictionary—and it was a real challenge to read fine print in the dim basement light.

When a teacher commented that we were "dumber than posts," we guessed she meant the one in our basement. "I know I'm smarter than that," I said to myself. I never got used to having the other children laugh at us, though, when we made mistakes. Often they poked fun at our accents and giggled at our garbled pronunciation. That hurt. We wanted to fit in with the other boys and girls, but sometimes the desire to disappear overwhelmed me.

Even in those dreary economic times, our clothes made us look ridiculous. Our pants were either too short, so that our knees hung out, or too long, so that we tripped on the fraying cuffs. What we wore frequently came from the thrift store; the clothes were worn and mended and baggy. To make matters worse, we often looked outdated and old-fashioned.

When we visited the boys' room it always took us a little longer because we were almost the only boys who still had buttons instead of zippers. I remember so clearly the titters that turned to belly laughs one afternoon as I tried to sit down after answering the teacher. Something was holding me up and preventing me from taking my seat. I followed the fingers pointing somewhere below my waist, and there saw a button caught between the upper lid and the base of the desk. I yanked hard and sat down quickly, my cheeks crimsoning with embarrassment. "Oh, boy," I thought with chagrin, "they'll get me on the playground for this!"

We couldn't connect with the other children because we had so little in common with them. We couldn't share stories about our family life because we recognized ours wasn't normal, and even if we had wanted to, Aunt Hildore wouldn't have allowed us to bring playmates into the house. Finally, we had no toys to share or trade.

Even if the other kids didn't understand why we were different, they must have realized the subtle ways in which our home life varied from theirs. Our school friends learned so much from dinnertime gossip, or when they went shopping, or visited their neighbors. Since Duane and I never had such normal experiences, we had nothing to add to conversations at recess, and we often tuned them out. We felt excluded when they recounted stories about family excursions—visits to the country or a cousin's farm after church on Sundays, and we certainly couldn't describe our afternoons spent in the basement. Even simple pleasures like family picnics seemed to be foreign and exciting events to us.

The one place where we fit in as normal boys was on the playground during games. Duane's keen eye-hand coordination meant he excelled in baseball, and he was one of the first to be picked when it came time to choose teams. Competition ran high in those games. At one recess just before the bell was due to ring, Duane came up to bat with one man on and a tie score. The pitcher wound up, and there was a satisfying thwack as bat and ball connected. Duane took off toward first, confident that he had a home run and a win for his side. Actually, no one could have fielded the hit, since it rose high as it left the bat. After sailing over the shortstop's head, it crashed with the unmistakable crack of breaking glass on the floor of our classroom. "You're going to get it, Duane," our classmates commiserated as the bell rang, and we filed back into the school with trepidation.

Corporal punishment was still permitted in those days, and the teacher sent Duane, as we had feared, to the principal's office. We were certain he would get the strap. How he avoided it still produces chuckles at our dinner table. He never made it as far as the office. On the way, he spied a rough patch of wallpaper that sparked an idea. Rubbing his hand on it just hard enough to produce some ugly red marks and wetting his cheeks and eyes at the water fountain to simulate a few tears, he returned to the classroom, supposedly chastised and chastened.

The other boys sympathized, and for a short while we enjoyed the satisfaction of being a part of their group. Unfortunately, though, our playground prowess didn't save us from unwanted attention from some of the meaner boys in the school as we walked home alone one day. One incident in particular stands out in my memory. A bunch of them, anxious to prove their superiority just because they were bigger—and didn't speak with accents—jumped us as we were walking home from Cromdale School. It wasn't a fair fight, six or seven of them against the two of us. After putting up as much resistance as we could and before we were too bloody and torn, we broke away. "Hurry up, hurry up," I yelled to Duane, just as he exhorted me, "faster, faster or they'll catch us!"

As if running for our lives, we tripped up the steps of the nearest house, anticipating safety as we punched the doorbell hard. To our immense relief an apron-clad woman opened the door almost immediately, but in our intense anxiety we jabbered our pleas for help in Swedish! It was still our first language—but not hers at all. *"Ni kan vänligen hjälpa oss*—can you please help us?" We stammered, *"Dessa pojkar är effter oss och de kommer slå oss*—those boys are after us, and they are going to beat us up!"

Not only could she not understand us, but she also thought we were just being a nuisance and trying to fool her. With a flourish of the feather duster she was holding, she exclaimed, "Off with you, you young ruffians. Don't you have anything better to do than bother an old lady trying to clean?" She slammed the door as we tried to offer an apology.

"Please, oh, please," we continued to beg. This time we spoke in English, but it was too late. We heard the latch click as she bolted the door, and then we turned to see the bullies gloating from the sidewalk in front of the next house. Somehow we got to our own back door, which was actually just down the block, without much further damage to our clothes or our egos.

Dad had heard the commotion and had come out, but he didn't try to stop the fight or save us from the bullying. Was he trying to make men of us by not interfering, or didn't he care? He was certainly bigger than any of the boys who began to slink away when they saw him. Looking back, I'm not sure I know the answer, but the next day Duane and I found a new way to walk home.

Chapter Nine
Waffles for Breakfast

After our experiences with foster families, we would usually stay in Edmonton for a few weeks or months until Dad could find someone else who was willing to take us, and these were by and large people who were looking for cheap labor. Driving back to Edmonton and peering at the two of us through the rearview mirror of his black 1939 Chevrolet, Dad would generally ask in a hearty voice, "How was it, boys?"

Maybe we were trying to forget about bad experiences, but we would try to tell about something good, especially if we had been treated fairly well. Perhaps, too, the memory of Aunt Hildore brushing off our complaints inhibited us from recounting more painful incidents. When we had been in the country, it was always safe to brag about what it was like to care for the baby chicks, or how many cows we could milk, or how many rows of runner beans we could weed in a morning after one of our farm stays.

"Hey, Dad," I remember one of us asking, "did you know that when the cows come home at night they know which is their own stall in the barn?" It didn't yet occur to us how strange it was that the farm animals had better living quarters than we did.

People who hear my story wonder why Duane and I never became bitter. I think what saved us from giving up were the few gentle and warm people who touched our lives. Some of the only enjoyable times we had while living in Edmonton were the weekends when we traveled with Dad to one of the churches in Clive or Lacombe. It was almost a ninety mile drive, so we always went the night before and slept at the home of one of the congregants. On the first trip we had few expectations, but to our great surprise the woman whose house we stayed at welcomed us immediately. Everything about her was round, from her ruddy cheeks smudged with a dab of flour and lips that curled upwards in a smile, to her ample waist covered with an immaculate white apron, to her dimpled arms that enfolded us before she had even heard our names. How surprised we were to discover there were women who liked to have little boys visit them and found pleasure in piling their plates high with steaming treats and special desserts.

I guess if we saw mothers buying presents for their children or enjoying their company, we thought it was unusual behavior, or maybe we looked away so we wouldn't compare other boys' lives to our own. At any rate, in Clive we got to take really warm baths upstairs with lots of soap, and the woman we stayed with even scrubbed our backs. We thought this was almost heaven. But what I liked best was that we each got our own towel. We didn't have to share a frayed and dingy terry cloth rag as we did in our basement home, and when we had finished bathing we would sleep in a real bed.

In the morning, after a big breakfast—we liked the waffles the best—we would get dressed in our Sunday clothes before walking to the small country church for early services. At nine o'clock Dad would preach, usually a fairly short sermon, and Duane and I would join in singing a duet. We still had the sweet voices boys usually lose by the time they are twelve or thirteen, so our musical contributions were appreciated. I wonder if that was a talent we inherited from our mother who we later learned was the finest soprano in the church choir.

Even if Dad had wanted to give a long sermon, he wouldn't have had the time, since on those Sundays we had to be in Wetaskiwin by noon when he would preach again. There would still be one more service when we got back to Edmonton, so those Sundays were long and a bit tiring, especially if we were expected to sing at night. Nevertheless, in the more relaxed atmosphere away from Aunt Hildore's scowling presence, I learned to appreciate the beauty of the liturgy and the resonance of the words of the King James Bible. I loved the soaring music as we intoned, "Holy, Holy, Holy is the Lord of hosts," and recited the comforting and familiar words of the Lord's Prayer. Even those Sundays when we had a communion service seemed shorter and more peaceful than when we were in Edmonton and had to sit with our aunt and cousins. Dad always treated us more strictly at those times, wagging a stern finger at us and calling us up to the front of the church if we talked during his sermon. If we escaped that embarrassment, Aunt Hildore would squeeze all of our arms so hard that even Linnea would angrily cry, "Quit pinching" to her mother. I think she was always surprised to be included in the punishment.

Unfortunately, those weekends in the country provided almost the only happy recollections we have of living with Dad. We had him all to ourselves since Aunt Hildore and the girls always stayed in Edmonton, and he relaxed on those weekends as he never could at home. I wonder now if he felt freer to be his own man and father us in a way that our aunt's presence prohibited.

Clive was also one of the few places where we made friends who didn't just play with us because we were in the neighborhood, but actually sought us out. There were three brothers—Frank, George, and Fernley—who would vie to have us stay with them and play. They were always fun to be with, especially in winter, when we would speed across the fields in their open sled pulled by a single horse. The boys would lend us extra clothes, and we would snuggle under warm robes as we watched the snowy landscape fly by. Eventually the cold would penetrate all those layers, but just as the chill was beginning to numb our toes, we would arrive back at their home for cookies and a hot drink. We finally learned what cocoa tasted like. But delicious as that was, we always saved enough room for dinner at the home of other parishioners, especially the Westling's. What a contrast those meals provided from the rigid meals we endured standing up and knowing how much our presence pained Aunt Hildore. Oscar Westling was a kind man.

Another heartwarming experience occurred when we drove to Wetaskiwin where there wasn't any church and the services took place in the Lutheran Home for the Aged. The elderly residents welcomed us warmly, since our young faces and active bodies were a refreshing change from the crotchety folks who surrounded them.

"Come over here, where I can see you better," someone would beckon, and we would try to be patient as bony fingers chucked us under the chin or smoothed down our cowlicks. Sometimes an elderly woman would reach into her worn handbag, poking into the deep recesses to locate a peppermint or other hard candy she had saved for us. We understood that they were just as lonely as we were and recognized how much they anticipated our visits.

After Dad's sermon, we would enjoy a late lunch at the courthouse, where a man named Aaronson was the custodian, and where inmates were housed in the jail. Finally, we would head back to Edmonton for vespers. By then we would be two sleepy boys nodding off in the back of the Chevy, but we were nevertheless refreshed from the loving attention we had enjoyed. Sometimes, I would take a last look at the black velvet sky with its galaxy of stars and wonder if I could touch them if I stretched my arms long enough. Those were the times I knew that one day I would live as I chose to, not confined to a dark cellar where the ceiling encroached on my dreams of seeing beyond the bleak present. Weekends away meant so much more than exposure to creature comforts and full bellies. They opened up possibilities of some day knowing human warmth and affection, things we wouldn't encounter again until adulthood. Food tasted better because we were treated decently, and I stored those memories deep in my psyche where they helped me survive later traumas.

Back in Edmonton and once again left to our own devices, Duane and I would often just meander along the streets, absorbing the sights and sounds, but not quite understanding why the city streets had grown more crowded and the faces of the people had grown increasingly cheerful. Everything amazed us, and nothing amazed us, since we lacked any frame of reference for what might seem either modern or out of date, and we just took whatever we observed at its face value. The arrival of the trolleys was one of the initial changes in Edmonton to intrigue me. They seemed to appear overnight in 1939 when they replaced the street cars that rode on tracks right past our house. Duane and I must have been in the country when the construction gangs ripped up the roadbed and erected the cables for the catenaries that fed power to the pantographs, the mechanical arms that guided the trams. I was fascinated by how smoothly the cars rode on their rubber tires, and because they were powered by electricity they left no fumes suspended in the air. I used to gaze at them wistfully as they glided down our street and around the corner. Sadly, I never got to ride on one of them. That was just another of the experiences that we were denied, while our cousins rode them whenever possible. Movies were another entertainment that Dad denied to us, saying that they were a bad influence and immoral. Duane and I could never figure out why this was true for us, but not for our cousins, who frequently bragged about the double features they had just seen.

Not having that opportunity also meant missing a valuable learning tool, for the newsreels shown between the features provided important information about World War II which Canada had entered in September 1939. The population of the city was just over 90,000 at that time, although with the construction of the Alaska Highway by American soldiers and the growth of the aviation industry, it would grow by almost 20,000 by the end of World War II. The city enjoyed a new prosperity, but the early euphoria that accompanied the influx of jobs dissipated as men shipped overseas and women took over their jobs. Most of this went over our heads since we were never allowed to listen to the radio either and Dad read his newspapers in his study. Ours was really quite an insular and provincial household—there was never any conversation about the turmoil in the world—at least not in our hearing.

Chapter Ten
Carlsons' Farm: The Early Years

We were only twelve years old in June 1943 when our aunt and uncle and the two girls took us out to Camrose, Alberta, to live with the Carlsons. They were a poor family who had two sons, Clifford and Florene, living with them. The boys were really grown men in their late twenties.

That first day, after Dad and Aunt Hildore left us around three o'clock in the afternoon, Florene asked, "Hey, fellows, how would you like to learn how to milk a cow?" He made it sound like an entertaining diversion even though he knew it would be part of our daily routine and not much fun on a cold winter morning. "Just watch me," he added, knowing it would take more than that for us to learn.

Next, he introduced us to the intricacies of getting water at the outdoor pump—not an easy task for our short arms because the pin that secured the handle frequently stuck, making it hard to crank. The windmill where we pumped water was almost 750 feet from the house, and although we were out of breath from our exertions, we had to carry the water to the house. Florene stood by, laughing at our attempts, but finally, after enduring his sarcastic laughs at our struggles mastering these new techniques, we heard Mrs. Carlson calling us to a supper of boiled food and no conversation. We were used to silent meals, and we were too tired to talk anyway. To our consternation we soon guessed that this was going to be the pattern of our days, and we went to bed that night with Duane asking, "I wonder how long we'll have to stay here—I hope it won't be very long."

I knew Duane resented being an orphan more than I did, and I was sometimes afraid he would get in trouble if he showed his anger. I remember consoling him, "We're just going to have to make the best of it and do what they expect if we want them to leave us alone. We'll take care of each other;

we're in this together; we've got to stick up for each other."

I realized already that we didn't dare talk back to any of the Carlsons, and we could only defend each other in private to avoid other repercussions. I had seen Florene clench his fists as Duane fumbled at the pump, and I could see he was itching to correct him with the back of his hand. The events of our first day didn't bode well for our future at the Carlsons' farm.

Years later we found out that Camrose was known as the rose of Alberta, but as I questioned Duane only recently, "Do you ever remember anything besides thorns at Carlson's farm?" There was simply no beauty in that life or even a quest for it. I guess Elna and Theodore—she called him Tither—were just too worn out by life by the time we arrived at their farm.

Like my father and uncle, Mr. Carlson had emigrated to the United States from Sweden, and he had moved to Canada in 1928 when he heard how fertile the land was for agriculture. Unfortunately, Mr. and Mrs. Carlson never prospered during the dust bowl years of drought and the Depression. Throughout most of the countryside, tractor power was replacing horse power, but the Carlsons had no modern conveniences. They had leased their farm for several years and had only recently saved enough money to purchase it from the Fridhem Lutheran Church which they attended.

Although both Elna and Tither had been born in 1887, their constant exposure to wind and rain, as they coaxed their meager livelihood from the earth, had aged them beyond their years. Elna's hair had turned that nondescript color that is neither gray nor white nor brown but just a streaked mixture of old age and fatigue. (I learned later that in the city they would call it salt and pepper.) We never saw her hair brushed out since it was skewered in the back in an untidy round bun, but long strands frequently escaped to hang in matted squiggles down her back.

Her skin hung from the bones on her face as if it was too tired to stick to them properly, and with her tall, spare frame she looked gaunt and gangly, rather than wiry and trim. Even in a rural community where women couldn't find much time to concentrate on their appearance, Elna's complexion looked as if it had been scrubbed with the same soap she used to scour her pots, and her hands were as rough as her cleaning brushes.

She wore the same washed-out cotton dress every day, or so we thought. She must have owned more than one, but they all looked identical because they had all bleached in the sun as they hung out to dry. She covered her mid-calf skirts with aprons made from the sack cloth that chicken feed and flour came in, and she would wipe her hands on these, leaving long stains from her household tasks or gardening jobs. Duane and I hadn't had much experience with pretty women, but we knew instinctively that Mrs. Carlson was quite plain. She frowned much of the time.

We never really felt we knew her well because as long as we finished our chores on time, she generally ignored us. However, after the first time we saw her kill a chicken, we realized we would be wise to stay on the right side of her. I had seen a lot of cruelty in the world, but I felt the gorge rise in my throat as I saw her wade into the flock of cackling hens and hook one of them around the neck with a long metal pole. She grabbed it with the other hand and with one violent twist wrung its neck. She looked ruthless and totally devoid of any feeling, and she seemed to enjoy the task.

By contrast, Cecelia, the Carlsons' only daughter, was a lovely looking young woman with soft curly hair who smiled frequently and always said hello to us. Some years ago she sent me a copy of a local history book that details the lives and customs of farmers in the Camrose area. In the article she wrote, she described how she used to soak and scrub and boil the lettering from the feed containers to make household bedding and linens. In fact, in some farmhouses every scrap of fabric came from those bags which were even printed with directions for the proper bleaching and included stitching lines for simple towels. She even created handkerchiefs from the salt bags.

I'm not sure why, but Cecelia's handiwork was much prettier than her mother's. It was probably in the details she added, like ruffles or pleats. She says she liked it even better when the flour started coming in bags with flowered prints or plaids and border prints because these could be sewn into attractive aprons and luncheon cloths. Cecelia certainly couldn't have inherited her eye for beauty from her mother; nothing at the Carlson farm was anything beyond utilitarian.

Cecelia lived almost five miles away with her husband, Elmer, and their daughter and four sons. We didn't see them often, but it was a good day when we spied them coming to visit in a wagon pulled by a matched pair of black horses. The sun seemed to shine brighter when they were in the house.

The last member of the Carlson family, son Raymond, had also gotten away from the farm and lived in town, where he worked at a lumberyard.

Tither resembled his wife, at least in his dour demeanor and in the roughshod way he treated most people. His conversations consisted mostly of one-word commands or grunts by way of a response—unless, of course, he was yelling at Duane or me to hurry up. I always think of him in the denim overalls he called his *byxors*, which is the Swedish word for pants. They started out clean every morning, but by the end of the day they were stiff with sweat, as was his thinning hair.

We went to the Carlson farm because Tither needed additional help on his farm. He was often away when he augmented his income with a second job, working with his friend Lutnus. The two of them traveled throughout the Camrose area refurbishing wooden pews and similar furnishings in churches and public buildings with their oak grain kits. The days were a little less stressful when he was gone, but it didn't mean we could slack off. There was no vacation from the needs of livestock, and Mr. Carlson would always check any other work he expected us to do.

The house, which might have been painted when it was new, was now a grayish white with bare patches of exposed wood; I can't remember if the roof was shingled with wood or just tar paper. It was really tiny, only 312 square feet, including the upstairs. When we arrived, I remember wondering where we would live in this house. Even now, I'll ask Duane, "How did we all fit into it?" That's probably why I recall so many of the measurements of the rooms. The downstairs living space was only about eight by ten feet, and it had a bed in one corner for Mr. and Mrs. Carlson.

When I looked closely, I could see that the faded old quilt had been sewn from once brightly colored remnants. There was a lumpy old couch that even the barn cats avoided if they snuck into the house and a single chair that might once have been decorated with cabbage roses. A little heat sometimes came from a coal-fired stove that did almost nothing to warm the place. In the frigid winters when the winds flattened the stubble in the wheat fields, the outside temperatures rarely rose above twenty degrees and frequently dropped between forty and fifty degrees below zero at night. It didn't feel much warmer inside the flimsy walls.

A rickety lean-to housed the kitchen where the Spartan furniture consisted of a trestle table and benches, with single chairs at the head and the foot. They had probably been bought as another housewife's proud choice when they first appeared in the old Sears Roebuck catalog that now served as toilet paper in the outhouse. Over time, the furniture pieces had been scrubbed and scoured until they were almost as white as the laundry should have been. The Carlsons had likely bid successfully on most of their furnishings at an auction, since they could afford to purchase almost nothing new. At some point, another room, only about eight feet by five, even smaller than the first, had been added on, and this was where Mrs. Carlson did her wash until we came to live there.

There was another space, only about ninety square feet, under the pitched roof that reached a height of only six feet. That was where Duane and I shared sleeping quarters with Florene and Clifford. The room would have suited Lilliputians better than it did us, and it would have induced nightmares in anyone claustrophobic.

At one end, the two of us slept on a single mattress (with no box spring) that measured a mere six feet by thirty inches. The mattress was so narrow we could hardly move, and it was impossible to turn over once we were both lying down. Whoever slept on the inside lay only inches from the side wall, and if he was sleeping on his back his nose almost poked into the roof struts. The bed— if I could call it that, since it was just a mattress on the floor— boasted only one lumpy pillow. Next to it was a miniature desk, and a storage box with a hinged lid. Our suitcase held our meager possessions. Florene and Clifford, who were much taller, had to kneel down to remove their clothes from the small cupboard they called their closet and an even smaller chest of drawers, and they dressed in an area no larger than three feet square. At least their mattress was considerably wider, and each of them had his own pillow. The farmhouse had been designed for strictly utilitarian purposes for people whose expectations of life were equally undemanding, and it was totally devoid of anything that resembled creature comforts.

In winter, with just dead space in the outer walls and no insulation there or in the bare rafters, the mercury frequently hovered around twenty-five degrees in the attic. Clad in our wooly long underwear, Duane and I appreciated each other's body heat when we crawled under our covers and hoped sleep would soon take our minds off the frigid air.

In the icy dawn, usually around five in the morning or whenever we heard Florene and Clifford stirring, we would leap up to go downstairs to dress. It would still be pitch-black, so we couldn't see our frozen breaths or the icicles hanging from the rafters. What little heat the pot-bellied stove gave out stayed in the room below for the door to the stairway was kept closed. In the morning, everything liquid was frozen to a solid block of ice. We would always be in a hurry to get to the outhouse, too. No one was anxious to go out there in the middle of the night in January or February.

Getting up at early light wasn't quite so bad in the spring or fall when the temperatures moderated, but in the summer the heat just curled itself around the eaves, and we woke up dripping sweat. Occasionally, cross-ventilation from the two windows afforded some relief if a breeze was blowing, but between the uncomfortable bed and the scorching heat or arctic temperatures, we only got through the nights at the Carlsons' farm because most boys can sleep through anything.

Once we were up and dressed, our workday began. The problem for Duane and me was that too many chores became our job. And most of them had to be finished before we went to school.

Time on a farm is often marked by unrelenting tedium, since schedules rarely change from day to day. Cows and pigs have to be fed at the same time, milking can't be skipped, stalls have to be mucked out, and while the chores may change by the season, the years are the same month after month.

On Mondays, I would walk out to the pasture to bring the cows back from the field where they had spent the night, and Duane would go into the barn to fill the manger with hay. On Tuesdays, we would reverse our roles. We never argued about whose turn it was, but just alternated our roles throughout the week.

During the three years we were at the Carlsons, the number of cows varied from nine to fourteen, although that depended on how close it was to slaughtering time. I am still amazed that those stolid, slow-moving bovines always remembered which was their own stall when they came in for the morning milking. They would wait for Duane or me to open the barn door, and then they would head right in to where they belonged. We had learned how to gently squeeze their udders to extract the milk on our first day there, but even when it became second nature and our hands had built up the necessary muscles and calluses, milking still took us forty-five minutes. The warm breath of the cows was welcome on a winter morning!

Once the milk was in the pail, we would pour it into the milk cans and head up to the house, where the separator was kept. Each can weighed about fifty pounds, but we somehow managed to carry or drag them. We were still too short to pour the milk into the bowl at the top of the separator and needed help from one of the Carlson sons. I always prayed it would be Clifford who would be available because he usually had a smile for us and a joke about small pints who couldn't reach too high. If it was Florene, he would change the same sentiment into a nasty comment if he thought quickly enough. He didn't much like being a farmer's son at that time and managed to take out his frustrations on us—and I think he was frustrated a lot of the time. At some point I learned that his twin sister had died when she was two after she was kicked by a horse. Maybe he sometimes felt he was only half a person, whereas Duane and I felt utterly complete.

Working at the separator we would once more take turns, turning the crank to separate the cream from the milk. Each would foam into its separate spout and then into its respective can. Next, there was more carrying to do since both the cream and the milk had to be stored in the ice house. The cream would go to the co-op on Saturday for sale, together with eggs all year around. (After the harvest there would be flax, barley, and wheat to take to the market as well.) The family used the rest of the milk for their meals and cooking.

When we finished with the milk we were pretty tired and ready for breakfast, but we still had one more chore to accomplish. Mr. Carlson might not know much about how to treat his workers, but he knew exactly what his livestock needed, so we had to feed the pigs before we could eat our own food. There were about twenty pigs that mostly ate scrapings from the family's plates and other leftovers. The Carlsons usually had one sow, but they had to bring in a boar from a neighbor's farm when they wanted to mate her.

Finally, it would be time to start the long walk to school. Our first school, called Thronson, was a long three miles away, and only seven students attended. After that closed, we went to the school where we met Wilbert Lyseng, one of the nicest boys we ever knew and a friend to this day. Besides Cecelia's family, Wilbert is probably the only good memory I have of Camrose, and we still talk occasionally.

The distance to Lyseng School was shorter as the crow flies, but since neither of us ever conquered flight, we had to walk a mile and a half around a pond and the belts of trees that sheltered the crops. Lyseng was a one-room schoolhouse with usually about eleven students in attendance, but even with such a small teacher-to-student ratio, our reading and arithmetic skills advanced slowly.

Based on today's statistics about the value of smaller classes, we should have learned quickly, but there was never any time or a suitable place for us to do our homework. Moreover, we never had any motivation to get ahead despite the efforts of our teacher, Mrs. French. She intimated she would help us after school, but we had neither the time nor the inclination to accept her offer. We had been exposed to so few people who had profited from education that we didn't understand how important it would be for us when we grew up.

The teacher at the Thronson schoolhouse, Mrs. Nesvold, was never able to motivate us either after we slogged through mud or snow or braved dry, searing winds following our morning chores. I can still see the boys and girls at the old wooden desks and hear us as we started each day singing "O Canada" (we never knew that we weren't Canadian citizens or that it wasn't truly our national anthem) or one of the popular hymns that everybody knew like "O God, our Help in Ages Past." We may not have thrived academically, but just the welcoming atmosphere of the teachers at each school nourished our minds and nurtured our spirits. My dreams of success, though severely tested, never quite died.

In winter, our trip to school was brutal in the extreme. I often say to Duane today, "It's a wonder we ever made it." He sometimes seems even more surprised than I do. Some of the coldest temperatures recorded in January and February in the 1940s dropped lower than fifty degrees below zero, yet we walked to school despite the weather and despite our lack of proper clothing. Neither Duane nor I ever had any winter boots for warmth even though we spent so much time outdoors. We each owned four or five pairs of socks which we wore every day. I think the Ladies' Aid Society knitted them, and some kind soul donated them to boys like us.

Since we didn't have the proper shoes to protect our feet, we laced Indian moccasins over our socks to keep out some of the chill. In the coldest months we didn't have to worry about getting wet feet, since the extreme cold kept the ground and snow frozen solid.

We never owned the right winter-weight jackets either, like the other boys wore, but insulated our skinny bodies with several layers of old sweaters that were probably left over from Clifford or Florene. We wound long scarves, also gifts from well-meaning others, round and round our necks and over our faces to prevent frostbite, and we covered our heads with hats with ear flaps.

By the time we were only a few feet from the Carlson house, ice would congeal on the scarves and coat our eyelashes and eyebrows as well. I'll bet we left a puddle on the schoolroom floor every morning as we thawed out!

"I hope there's a good fire in the school stove," I muttered each day as we started out on our trek, and sometimes I can almost still smell our wet wool mittens and leggings hanging up to dry by that stove. I guess other kids could smell us, too. As we defrosted, the aroma of kids like us who only took baths on Saturday nights and wore the same clothes to school every day must have been very noticeable. I never realized that other kids might have found us offensive in that way, but I'll bet we weren't the only boys with that once-a-week habit. The jingle that "Life Buoy stops B. O." might have been coined just for us. We used to hear that advertisement for one of the most popular and earliest deodorant products on the mass market when Mr. Carlson listened to his radio.

What might have caused us more embarrassment, had we known better, was our lack of dental hygiene, or more accurately stated, our lack of toothpaste. We never had any. The only provision we had for cleaning our teeth was a small portion of salt that we applied with the end of a wet fingertip. We were ignorant of another well known radio ad, "You'll wonder where the yellow went…" for we had certainly never heard of Pepsodent toothpaste. In fact, the first time we ever visited a dentist was after we enlisted in the navy, and by that time our teeth were in dire straits with monumental amounts of decay.

I'm sure the watered-down milk Aunt Hildore had given us at breakfast when we were growing up contributed to our oral problems, and the long hours we spent working in the sun didn't quite compensate for an early lack of vitamin D. Such thoughts were far from our minds, however, as we shivered in the warm schoolhouse, our bodies gradually adjusting to the room's temperature.

Possibly the only things that actually kept us from freezing to death on our trek to school were the snow caves we learned to dig on our way to Thronson and Lyseng. In the early winter on a Saturday when our chores were done, Duane and I would hollow out deep trenches in the snow drifts piled high along the roadway where the plows had cleared. I've seen websites that give directions on the best way to construct a snow cave, but we didn't have any instructions to guide us. I think our commonsense indicated that any protection from the wind would literally be a lifesaver, and so we just burrowed as deep as we could into the snow banks. We huddled in them until we felt warm enough to brave the winds and forge ahead again. No wonder we never really liked school, since it was such torture to get there!

When spring thaws finally came, we had to hop from rut to rut to prevent our feet from sinking into the mud. During those weeks we wore rubber boots, the same ones we wore when we cleaned the barn and the hog houses. I'd guess our teacher made sure those stayed outside the schoolhouse door! The walk was unpleasant, but at least we didn't suffer from chilblains. I still can't understand why Florene wouldn't let us ride his horse on the worst of days.

In our final year at the Carlsons, our uncle took pity on us and bought us a bicycle. Most of the time it was either too icy or too muddy for it to do us much good, but when we could ride it, we devised a unique way to maneuver. We would take turns, one sitting on the bicycle seat and the other on the crossbars, helping to peddle. "My turn," we would remind each other when the metal began to dig into our bony backsides. What a comical sight we must have been as we wobbled down the road, weaving back and forth!

By the time we got back to the farmhouse after school at five o'clock, we had to face the same monotony of work we had completed in the morning— forking the hay, milking the cows, and feeding the pigs. The only difference at the end of the day was that the cows could wend their own way from the barnyard back to the fields. It's no wonder we gave our homework little or no thought.

In the spring of 1942, one of the sows had a litter of piglets, and as so often happens, one poor little piglet turned out to be a hapless runt. Florene had no sympathy for any creature weaker or smaller than he was, especially if he could foresee no monetary value in it, so when he saw the tiny pig, he grabbed it by its hind legs and flung it against the side of the pen. I still shudder when I recall its mewling and squealing as it lay helplessly in the muck, its little ribs almost sticking through the lacerations in its flesh. "That'll take care of that useless creature," Florene muttered, nudging the shuddering body with his toe.

"Oh, Florene," we cried, "if she's no good for the farm, can't we have her?" He looked disgusted that we would consider caring for such a poor specimen of porker, but he agreed, adding cruelly, "Go ahead; it will just be dead in the morning."We took the pig into the barn finding a space for her where she wouldn't get stepped on. We treated her with the "bag balm" that we used on the cows' teats when they cut themselves on barbed wire. We named her Susy.

Each morning after we had finished feeding her more robust brothers and sisters, we would bring her warm milk, letting her suck it from our fingers. We also strained grain for her, making a mild gruel that she could digest easily. We marveled at how well she grew, and we congratulated ourselves on her remarkable progress. Soon we built her a special pen of her own near the barn.

By the time she was eight months old she had developed into a real specimen of a healthy pig. We mentally patted ourselves on the back for our skills at animal husbandry when we visited her after school. She sensed our arrival, and as we got close to her she would squeal and rub against the fence. In the morning, she would ignore us as if she knew we were going off to school and wouldn't be back to see her all day.

Alas, others noticed how successful we had been in raising her. One day we found her little sty empty. When we questioned Florene if he knew where she was, he merely shrugged and answered, "She must have run away." We were too intimidated by him to verbally doubt his reply, but we knew instinctively what had happened to her. Like the little piggy in the nursery rhyme, our Susy had gone to market.

Chapter Eleven
Carlsons' Farm: Boys Working Men's Jobs

Life at the Carlson farm was primitive in the extreme for the 1940s, when most people depended on electricity and had quickly adapted to modern conveniences, even in the country. Kerosene lamps were our only source of light. They gave off a weak, yellow glow that illuminated just a few feet of the room and accentuated the dark corners. A windmill several hundred feet from the house provided all our water. With its latticed frame and whirring blades, it was also the only graceful object on the farm.

Three times a day, either Duane or I had to trudge with buckets from the windmill to the house to get enough water to satisfy the needs of six people. I don't like to whine, but that took a lot of energy, and we had other strenuous tasks every day. We were only eleven years old when we first met the Carlsons, and we weren't big kids yet. Farm work is tough for anyone, but we were still quite short when we arrived in Camrose, and that made most of our chores even harder. Since we had to rely on the horses for field work and local transportation, it was imperative that we overcome the challenge of harnessing and bridling Jerry and Fly. They were old and good-natured, and, like most draft horses, they had been bred for heavy tasks such as plowing. They were patient and had docile temperaments. They were also big, somewhere around seventeen or eighteen hands and well over 1,000 pounds. Getting them ready to pull the wagon or other equipment would take us a little while to learn, but Mr. Carlson was impatient. "Don't know how to do that, yet?" he'd growl. We knew we needed to learn quickly. It's too bad, I think now, that he didn't have as much patience as his own horses.

One of the first tricks we mastered involved feeding the horses a bucket of oats to get their heads down so we could slip on the bridles. Even standing on a box, neither of us was quite tall enough to get the horses ready by ourselves. One of us would hand over the harness, and together we would throw it over the horse's back. Then we would have to wrap the neck collar of the harness round Jerry's or Fly's head, securely fastening the clasps. To fasten the nose and chin strap and to slide the bit into the horse's mouth took a lot of practice. We had to stretch up on the tips of our toes to pull the ears through the proper openings. After much maneuvering, pulling, fastening, and tightening all the equipment, we would be ready to thread the reins through the collar and lead the horse out by the bridle.

We eventually developed a method of teamwork to transform our bumbling efforts into skilled motions, but we relied on the horses' good natures to stand by resignedly while we improved. Only by a quick swish of their wiry tails did they ever indicate that they might be thinking, "Can't those boys hurry up so we can get moving?"

After we had been living on the Carlson farm for about a year, we worked out an ingenious method of hauling the water by redesigning an old stone boat. This was a sled-like contraption mounted on logs instead of runners, and often homemade, that was popular in the western United States and Canada for hauling bales of hay and large rocks.

"Hey, Ed," Duane suggested, "why don't we pump the water into that fifty-gallon barrel and then we can drag it on the boat to the house?" Duane was frequently our ideas man—and he had the dexterity to follow through on his thoughts. We soon discovered that there was a major problem in the way the conveyance had been built. Two parallel logs were attached to one another by horizontal planks, with a hook at the front that was attached so Fly could pull it. However, when the horse started to drag the sled, the pressure on the hook caused the whole contraption to buckle in the center and threatened to capsize the barrel and spill the water.

Together Duane and I figured out that if we used two hooks, attaching each to the parallel pieces, we could balance the apparatus safely. Also, the Carlsons had never considered shaving the front of the logs so that they could move like runners on a sled. Once we had solved that piece of the puzzle, we were in business. After scrubbing and scouring the barrel so the water stayed clean enough to wash the clothes, we had perfected our water transportation system. Unlike the rest of the family who went to town on Saturday nights and had baths at Raymond's apartment, Duane and I had to rely on our own efforts to secure water. Our invention made it much easier to keep our bathtub full.

Monday through Saturday, we were never at a loss for activity. During the three years we lived with the Carlsons, there wasn't a farm chore we didn't learn to master. Nevertheless, we were treated more like slaves than hired hands, and, it must be remembered, in those days most hired hands were grown men, not young boys. If we thought we had worked hard at any other place we'd lived, this was where we really learned the meaning of manual labor. Mostly what we were aware of at first was how immensely tough our lives had become—and it hadn't been easy before.

Today when I want a cup of coffee, I marvel at the ease with which I fill my cup from an instant hot water source. That would have been a luxury for us in Alberta, where we had no gas lines or propane tanks for instant fuel but just a cantankerous old wood stove that Mrs. Carlson used for cooking. To keep a monster like that at working capacity required prodigious amounts of kindling and logs, and we'd barely been in Camrose two months when Mr. Carlson warned us, "You boys think the cows and pigs take a lot of time? That there stove eats trees like you won't believe, and from now on you're in charge of the wood pile."

I know some people fantasize about sitting in front of the fire, maybe toasting marshmallows, with the logs crackling and hissing and the flames casting shadows on the faces of the perfect family. Some even romanticize hiking into the forest to fell a tree and triumphantly cart it back to their vacation home with enough lumber to fill their antique stove or a facsimile they have discovered in a glossy catalog. But, for the two of us, cutting was never anything but plain, hard, sweaty work.

Usually Clifford or Florene would take us out to the stand of trees in August to choose a full-grown birch to chop for firewood. That was the easy part. After selecting the tree, we would have to hitch up Fly, whose muscle power was an integral part of our farm labor. With a chain wrapped around one end of the log and with a smart smack on Fly's flanks, we would urge her forward. She didn't much like that—it was just as hot for her as it was for us—and she wasn't really used to working for us that first summer. Sometimes we would have to grab her by the bridle and tug her forward until the chain was taut. Slowly, she would move ahead until we could see the muscles strain in her sturdy legs and the blood vessels in her necks protrude like thick coils. "Ho, Fly, ho," we would encourage her as she labored to pull her heavy burden.

Next we would cut the wood into manageable pieces about 14 to 16 inches long, and then we had to learn how to split them. I imagine it's kind of fun to split just enough wood for the occasional campfire, visualizing oneself as a modern-day Paul Bunyan. But in order to provide enough wood for our hungry stove, we had to master the art of splitting it quickly—and in huge quantities.

First, we found a large round tree stump to use as a chopping block, and after placing a cut piece on its end, we learned to stand so that we could swing the ax with straight arms, hitting the wood right in the center. It soon became clear that if we hit on the side of the wood closest to us, we would drive the blade right into the ground, dulling it in just a few strokes. Florene became livid when that happened. On the other hand, if we hit on the far side, the ax handle might hit the stump. "Damn you boys," Florene would yell if he saw us doing that, "you want me to take a new ax handle out of your wages?" "That will be the day," I murmured under my breath, "he never pays us anything anyway."

As I got better at splitting wood, I would stand with my legs apart, pull the ax straight back over my head and swing it forward. A resounding crack would fill the air when Duane and I did this properly, but it took us dozens of tries before we gained any dexterity. Too often, we had insufficient speed or strength in the beginning, and then we would have to wrestle the hatchet from the wood when it got stuck. It was helpful to have a twin brother on hand when that happened. However, we also learned to stand back when the other was wielding the ax if we didn't want to get hit by flying chips or a loosened ax head! With just a few gentle hits into the crack to separate remaining strands of wood, we would have a few short pieces—maybe enough for the stove to fry an egg.

Each summer, with the heat frequently around eighty degrees, we would initiate this back-breaking process. I can still feel the rivers of sweat that would plaster my hair to my skull under my cap and stream down, stinging my eyes, sometimes obscuring my aim. I didn't dare let go of the ax handle to wipe the sweat away, for fear it would be my shin that would get split!

That was just the beginning of the battle, as we soon found out. There was also an art to constructing the wood pile. We would take the newly cut pieces to make a circle about two feet high and twenty feet in diameter and then filled the center until it reached about five feet, a grueling task for two guys who weren't much taller than the stack itself.

We went through this process twice by the end of each autumn to ensure we had enough tinder for the kitchen stove to last through the long winter. By the time we had finished, we had processed between thirty and forty cords each year, but by that point we were too exhausted to be impressed by our accomplishment.

Washing one load of clothes was another gargantuan task that Duane and I soon found on our long list of chores, and Mrs. Carlson's washer was no Maytag like Aunt Hildore used in her basement. First, we had to pump the water from the windmill and carry it, walking crookedly to one side as we were weighed down by the heavy bucket. We tried to walk slowly, taking great care to hold the pail steady. Whatever we spilled, we had to replace on a second or third trip to end up with enough water. In hot weather the cold drips felt good on our hot legs, but once autumn came, our skin would pop out in goose bumps from an icy splash. Our redesign of the stone boat after that first year saved us a lot of grief as well as a lot of effort, and it speeded up the process.

The washtub was a round, wooden, barrel-like structure supported on legs with an external wheel to turn the agitator. Back and forth, forth and back, we had to pull on the mechanism that resembled an upside-down stool attached to the inside of the lid of the washer. I was glad to have a twin, because when I complained that I thought my arms were falling off from the exertion, Duane would take over. Again, our short stature made the job so much more difficult since we couldn't get the proper leverage for a smooth motion. But we strained away because we had learned the hard way what happened when we failed.

It didn't matter to either of the Carlsons that a pair of wet jeans weighed almost fifty percent more than the same pants when Theodore took them off to go to bed. The laundry was now our job. It took an arduous ten minutes to wash a load and then another ten minutes to rinse, and when we had wrung the clothes as dry as our tired muscles could get them, we hung them on the clothesline. Their frozen shapes looked frighteningly grotesque in winter! Our hands looked the same.

Although we could move a little more slowly on Saturday mornings because we didn't have to rush off to school after breakfast, Mr. Carlson or one of his sons would always have a mental list of tasks for us.

"Looks like this would be a good day to get that fence fixed," one would announce through a mouthful of porridge. Thus, the day would start with unrolling the barbed wire and pulling it taut with a wire stretcher, another job that we could only finish if we worked together, each of us straining to overcome the resilience of the fencing. If we had to dig the postholes, we would stand on either side of the handle to turn the augur. By throwing all our weight into our efforts, we could slowly turn it until eventually the shaft reached the proper depth.

Just recently as Duane and I shared lunch, we commiserated about our early days, saying to one another, "I don't know how we ever made it." But as a united team, make it we did, and we only grew stronger for it, both physically and emotionally.

Chapter Twelve
Carlsons' Farm: Fruits of Our Labor

We never stayed out of school for chores, but during harvest season, kids were excused from attending in order to assist their families and neighbors wherever they were needed. It was essential for the farmers to use that small window of time when the wheat was ripe and the weather cooperated to get their crops in before the first frost destroyed the grain.

By the 1940s when we farmed in Camrose, combines had mostly replaced horse-drawn reapers except on the most backward or poorest spreads. It was our misfortune to live on one of those farms. Duane and I were never really strong enough to contribute much to this annual effort, but we faced this project with our usual sense of cooperation. The Carlsons rarely recognized our compliance. The harvest the year we were thirteen is forever etched in my memory.

"Get up you lazy louts," an angry voice roused us, and someone grabbed my arm, yanking me from a deep sleep. The first rays of the sunrise were streaking the attic floor, and in the early light we could just make out that Clifford and Florene's beds were already empty. We must have overslept! We had tumbled onto the mattress bone weary the previous night, exhausted from laboring in the field.

As I pulled myself up, trying to avoid Mr. Carlson's angry glare, I thought as I often did, "It's not what he expects of us. It's the way he jerks us around. Lots of boys work hard. But couldn't he ever act a little bit grateful for all we do?" Everybody appreciates a little gratitude, and a smile is worth a thousand commands, but the old man always behaved as if he had gotten up on the wrong side of the bed. We had learned never to express such ideas out loud though, so we got dressed and tended to the cows and pigs.

Jerry and Fly must have been just as tired. They had spent the previous day pulling the harvest binder that cut the grain and then bundled it into thirty or forty pound lots that only the older boys could manage. Duane and I struggled to drag the bundles to where the others would gather them together in stooks, but it was more than we could accomplish. We were lucky if we could just get them to stand up.

On large farms the stooks protected unthreshed hay or straw from moisture until it could be picked up. In a small operation like ours, the harvest could be completed in a day or two. Mr. Carlson relied on his son-in-law to provide what little machinery he allowed. Elmer Olson would spend a few hours operating his steam tractor to run the threshing machine (also his) that separated the grain. In most areas, steam tractors had been phased out by the mid-1920s in favor of internal combustion engines. But in this, as with most modern techniques, the Carlson farm was hopelessly outdated.

After the grain was deposited in the wagon, the horses would again be pressed into service to pull it to the huge granary near the barn. Duane and I were able to take over at that point to manipulate a somewhat archaic gasoline engine and move the wheat up the chutes and into the bins for storage. One of the photographs we have from this period, which Elmer or Cecelia took, shows Duane standing tall in the wagon, as if he was balancing on a seat. He was really perched on top of a pile of wheat, which indicates how much we gathered in a day.

Sometime about mid-morning, Clifford would start pulling his watch out of his bib overalls, as if willing the hands to signify noontime and lunch. Finally, satisfied that the food would be ready, he would wave his hand to Elmer, and we would all pile into the wagon and return to the house.

Mrs. Carlson always left a basin of water on a table outside so we could wash off the dust, and grit, and grain that clung to our sweaty faces and necks before going in to eat. Funny, even though the family never missed church, we never offered a blessing or a prayer of thanksgiving before we delved into a meal.

In some communities the harvest is celebrated with a great festival, but if there was one in Camrose, we never participated. I have even read there is a popular celebration in Wetaskiwin where Dad used to preach. Among the most highly regarded displays are the the smoking, chugging, massive steam tractor engines. They are billed as "the real crowd-pleasers of this show." I get a kick out of knowing that what we considered hopelessly old-fashioned (yet a boon to fulfilling our tasks) is thought of as entertainment for people today. Such joy was never part of life at the Carlson farm.

Since Mr. Carlson's personality was a cross between cantankerous independence and sheer cussedness, he didn't collaborate with the neighbors unless circumstances forced him to. However, because it was common practice for several farm families to go together to purchase a cow to provide beef for the table, slaughtering the animal was a joint venture. It wasn't a pretty sight, and after my first experience I tried to avoid it. Several men would tie the animal, and it required a lot of heft to suspend it from a tripod so it would bleed out properly after its throat was cut. Everyone ceased working when that was accomplished and retired to the kitchen to devour the blood pancakes that Mrs. Carlson would cook. They were a treat for most of the men, but I have always been revolted even by their name. "I'd rather go hungry," I'd say to Duane, and he would agree. There wasn't enough room for us at the table anyway with all the guests, so no one missed us.

In my photo album I have a picture that shows Duane after he had stumbled into a beehive or hornets' nest. I can't remember what we were doing when it happened, although it might have been during the threshing, but all of a sudden a great swarm of insects burst angrily around him, attacking and stinging him all about his face and neck. The Carlsons' reaction reminded me of the time Duane was scalded by the bath water at Grandahls, and their medical treatment was similarly antiquated. Mrs. Carlson daubed a little baking soda on his welts, and without attempting to remove any stingers or clean his sweaty skin, she sent him back out to finish his work. "You'll survive," she commented. She was never one to indulge in consoling remarks, but since we had so seldom encountered any comfort from her or anyone else, her lack of concern barely registered with us. Duane's usual good health sustained him, and he healed without scars—God had blessed both of us with a strong constitution, for we never once visited a doctor while we were youngsters.

However, this was the second time Duane had suffered serious injury while working for other families, and it became the catalyst for one of the few times we discussed running away as we grew older. We were alone in the attic for once and free to talk out of Clifford or Florene's hearing. Ever the practical one, Duane queried, "How would we get away from here? Where would we get food?" We both recognized the futility of trying to hitch a ride with anyone to get away from the Carlsons—everyone knew us and would ask where we were going. There was never any extra food at the farm, so if we wanted to eat, we'd have to find a way to steal it. Such an act was so far from Dad's teaching and our moral code that we quickly abandoned any further conversation about escaping. Dad had always set a very high bar for our behavior, and we continued to measure our actions against it until we were grown men.

About the only time we could enjoy time to ourselves were Saturday nights when the Carlsons usually left the farm after supper. They never included us in their outings, and they didn't want us to know what they were doing either. They slyly discussed their plans, secretly they thought, until one day when Dad paid a visit that had some unexpected consequences. Elna and Tither overheard Duane and me talking in Swedish to our uncle, as we usually did when we were alone. It had never occurred to the Carlsons that we spoke the language they had so often used to disparage us, thinking their comments were going over our heads.

"You mean the boys understand Swedish?" they questioned Dad, immediately regretting all the times they had made their Saturday night plans when they thought we couldn't understand them. "Of course," he responded. That ended the days of their supposedly mysterious conversations. There wasn't much to laugh about at the Carlson farm, but that provided one of our rare moments of humor. It feels good to outsmart the bully, especially when he's bigger.

The Carlsons weren't particularly religious, but Sundays always started with the service at Fridhem Lutheran Church, and we went to that in the old wagon pulled by Jerry and Fly. It was really just a large farm cart with no seats, so everybody stood in it and hung onto the sides. That was how we traveled in all weather, even rain and snow, although we did at least have an umbrella for inclement days.

From late September until April, the roads were covered with drifts but were never plowed, and we rarely saw the bare ground in that period. During that time, the wagon box would be taken off the wheel base and suspended on runners. The fences were often buried more than a foot below the top of the snow, but somehow the horses knew where the road was and made their own path, so the family never missed worship regardless of the conditions. It's a miracle Jerry and Fly never stumbled into the barbed wire. That sleigh ride didn't compare favorably with the one in Clive.

Everyone else arrived in cars, but Mr. Carlson was too cheap to drive the one and a half miles distance to hear Pastor Bernardson, and he said he needed to save his gasoline coupons for his other work with Lutnus. The only other time he used the old Pontiac (which Duane and I called his *Pontenac,* since our English was still faulty and we weren't completely weaned from Swedish) was to drive his cream and eggs the six miles to the co-op.

On Sundays, our only responsibility was caring for the livestock, so after we had eaten our noonday dinner we basically had the rest of the day to ourselves. In good weather, we would spend the time trapping gophers and killing crows, for they were worth good bounty money. We could get five cents for every ten gopher tails or set of crow's claws we turned in, a small fortune for us, and our trapping was a boon to the neighboring farmers. In addition to the diseases the gophers carried, their holes were dangerous for horses to step in, and everyone hated the crows for the seed and crops they devoured.

If we couldn't entertain ourselves doing that, we frequently felt bored and would often complain to one another, "Wouldn't you think Florene would let us ride his other horse, Noble, once in a while?"

We had begun to realize that our presence benefited all the Carlsons in other ways than just the workload we carried. Our semi-permanent residence with them meant that they had the use of our ration coupons each month. By 1943, everyone felt weary and tired of coping with food shortages imposed by World War II, and although we had probably enjoyed better fare than city dwellers, some commodities were scarce for everyone. Shortages of food and the rationing of so many goods, from lard and flour to meat and gasoline, brought the fighting to our doorstep as each night we listened to the newscasts on the family's battery-operated radio.

The combat we heard about nightly seemed far off, but we also had our own private hostilities. Take the allocation of our sugar. Each month, Mrs. Carlson divided the family's allotment evenly, with each person's portion measured into a glass labeled with his or her name. We could eat it all at once or spread our share evenly throughout that time period. Equitable as this might seem, it didn't work quite as planned, because when Florene or Clifford found his glass was empty, he simply helped himself to ours. We were much too smart to put up any opposition to that ploy, since the boys were much bigger and meaner than we could hope to be.

Chapter Thirteen
Carlsons' Farm: Deliverance

We had adjusted to Mr. Carlson by the time we had spent two years at the farm. We had learned to ignore his scathing yells, (*dumbom*, Swedish for fool or idiot) whenever we made a mistake or were slow learning something new. After all, we had both developed pretty thick skins after living with Aunt Hildore's abuse. Even so, I was horribly surprised at what happened to us on our last Christmas with the Carlson family.

The Carlsons had developed a simple method of disposing of the wastewater from the dishes or laundry that was efficient, but messy. Instead of taking the bucket out to the back of the house to dump it, they would just open the kitchen door and, standing in the entry, toss the contents about six feet away. In warm weather, the water would soak into the ground, although the area could become a mud hole after a heavy rain or thaw. In winter, it became quite treacherous, and we learned to step carefully when it froze. However, on Christmas Day, as he was coming back to the house from the outhouse, the old man (that's what Duane and I privately called him) didn't notice that the slops had frozen. Maybe he was carrying a load of wood and couldn't see above it, or maybe he just wasn't watching where he was going. I remember hearing him curse as he started to slide, and then there was an almighty crash as he fell.

He didn't break anything, but he sure was bruised. He needed a scapegoat to soothe his wounded feelings so, of course, he made us the culprits. He didn't like to look foolish in front of Clifford and Florene or even us. With a roar that reminded me of Mr. Grandahl's awful temper, he rounded on us, screaming, "*Dumbom, dumbom!* You idiots! You'll pay for this! So you think you are going to eat a fine Christmas dinner with us? No, you'll be lucky if you get any!" With that he sent us rushing below to the root cellar. "And don't you make a sound," he warned. "Cecelia and Elmer are bringing their children for dinner, and I don't want to hear a peep from you or you'll have to sleep down there!" Since we had gone to Edmonton the year before for the holiday, he knew no one would ask where we were.

We crouched amid the drying roots that had been hanging from the ceiling for years, their original purpose long forgotten. Rows of beans and tomatoes and other produce Elna canned each year filled shelves that looked like they might collapse on our heads. Cobwebs, more ancient than the herbs that turned to powder when we touched them, filled the corners. Dead bugs and other litter covered the hard earthen floor.

It was pretty creepy down there—without Duane's presence to comfort me, I wonder if I could have kept my feelings of hopelessness and despair at bay. Yet it wasn't really the physical surroundings that were so frightening in those moments, but the overwhelming loneliness that washed over me. I was enveloped in a darkness that threatened to seep into my soul.

At times like these, I was so grateful for my twin who was surely my other half. We wrapped our arms around our torsos, hugging first ourselves, and then each other, to keep from shivering. When we could bear the cold no longer, we called up, "Could we have a coat?" Carlson must have realized how frigid it was down there, because someone threw down a jacket to keep us warm and a candle so we could see. And that is how we spent Christmas 1944.

How sad that the day on which children celebrate the birth of the baby Jesus with expectation and joy—the day most boys and girls consider the highlight of their year—represented for us some of the bleakest times of our lives. There was the terrible Christmas Eve of the robber, and the previous Christmas had been a dreadful experience when we had gone from the Carlsons back to Edmonton for the holiday. Now, as Duane and I huddled into the meager warmth of the jacket in the root cellar, I must have dozed, for I found myself reliving the despair of that sad holiday at Dad's.

At that point in our lives, we still didn't know much about celebrations, but we had gleaned some idea about family festivities from the radio and from what we saw in store windows or the Sears Roebuck catalog. The Carlsons occasionally ordered from Sears when they needed something the stores in Camrose didn't carry, but mostly we only had a chance to look at old copies of the catalog in the outhouse. By that time, random pages had been ripped out to be used for toilet paper, so our images of Christmas were quite incomplete. They generally were tattered replicas of Santa Claus or a toy train with a picture of an engine that probably appeared on the next page. Between our ignorance of what constituted yuletide joy as well as the wartime shortages, we didn't entertain any visions of sugarplums. That was a good thing, since there were never any for us.

I don't know why we'd gone home that previous year during the Christmas vacation, but that season remains one of my saddest memories. As I was growing older, my sensitivities were also developing, and I was becoming aware of my needs even when I couldn't put words to them. That Christmas I felt an emptiness that I hadn't known earlier.

As usual, Aunt Hildore sent us to our cellar quarters as soon as Dad drove us to the house. There, in a crack in the concrete floor, we found a branch from the family's tree that Dad had trimmed. On the "tree" hung a few foil icicles and two apples and two oranges. These were our only decorations; they were our only presents as well.

What hungry boys we were, how starved for affection and signs of love that we found solace in such a pitiful sight. We were so deprived of beauty we assured each other that the tree was nice, and we relished the taste of the fruit as if it were a delicacy. We were even grateful that we didn't have to eat the core of the apple as we did at the Carlsons' on the rare occasion when we dared to ask for one. The only part we were allowed to discard there was the stem.

For the rest of that stay, Duane and I could hear the family above merrily laughing and someone, maybe Miriam, singing. Occasionally, we could also hear them listening to Christmas carols on their radio. A few smells of the holiday baking wafted down when they opened the door on the landing.

Although we had still never experienced the excitement of sharing this wonderful time with anyone, we knew instinctively that it was unnatural for us to be so cut off from human feelings and relationships. As we grew older, this knowledge was beginning to intensify. Nevertheless, we rarely made comparisons between those festive sounds and the murkiness and silence we endured—to do so would have been too discouraging, so we continued to tolerate what we couldn't change. No wonder that today I revel in yards and yards of garland and twinkling lights, silvery ribbons, and a table laden with rich fruitcakes and imported chocolates. Despite this, Christmas is not a happy time for me. There are too many memories, none of them good.

The last year at the Carlsons' we had a little leisure time, for we could finish the chores more quickly now that we were stronger. We spent hours listening to the radio in front of the window in the main room where it got the best reception and enjoyed this respite from our rather monotonous lives. Despite the lack of electricity, farmers like Carlson were able to buy battery-operated sets for about eighteen dollars, and these farm radios, as they were called, provided a valuable link to the world's happenings.

We didn't care so much about the news, but we loved *"Get Back in the Saddle Again"* with Gene Autry, and we thrilled to the sound of *"The Shadow."* The memory of Lamont Cranston's ghostly, echoing cackle still sends a pleasurable chill down my spine, although Duane never wanted to listen to that program. He said it gave him a different kind of chills.

The summer when we were fourteen, I enjoyed a bit of a reprieve when the Nesvolds, who farmed adjoining acreage, invited me to stay with them. I overheard Mrs. Nesvold, who was a cousin of our former teacher, explaining to Elna, "Our hand has been feeling poorly during this hot weather, and it would sure be a help if Edwin could come do a bit of helpin' out fer us." I spent two weeks there, and the Nesvolds kindly loaned me their horse so I could visit Duane, who was still working at Carlsons' and feeling lonely without me. At that point in our lives, we had never been apart.

I knew the Nesvolds were decent people since I had observed how they acted toward other kids when we saw them at church, and I think they knew how rotten our lives had become. I liked working there, not because Mrs. Nesvold didn't expect me to do the work of ten men, but because her face would light up with approval at the sight of a job well done. She would hum to herself as she puttered around the kitchen making apple dumplings—what a treat they were—and even added a pat on the back when she was pleased. It was a wonderful environment, and Mrs. Nesvold was one of the happiest employers I ever had. The only sadness in her life was the absence of her son, who had joined the army when Canada went to war in 1939.

I will never forget the steamy August day when I was out trying to stook wheat sheaves, and she appeared, waving me to stop. "Edwin," she gushed, her words spilling out. "you won't believe it! You just won't believe it. The war is over!" Tears spilled from her eyes as she spoke, and I knew her thoughts were far away with the son who had left so long ago for the European theater.

"Oh, Mrs. Nesvold," I told her, "he'll be home tomorrow!" As I recall, my abysmal ignorance of both geography and the military brought the glimmer of a smile to her lips.

Our years at the Carlson farm might have extended indefinitely, but shortly after that conversation with Mrs. Nesvold, our tenure came to an abrupt end when Dad paid a visit. He was probably delivering one of the monthly checks, and I think he might have come a day earlier than usual because he wasn't expected. At any rate, Duane and I were hard at work by ourselves when he arrived. We were doing our best to dig the basement for a new addition to the farmhouse, using the scoop pulled by Fly. Dad was horrified, since it was clear neither of us was big enough or strong enough for the task.

"Boys," he asked, "is that required of you?" He didn't say more except, "I'll be back in a week." True to his word, he returned seven days later and tersely commanded, "Boys, get your things. We're going home."

That was the last we saw of the Carlsons, and I have often wondered how they managed without us. That was also one of the few times that Dad seemed to recognize what an unfair life he had imposed on us.

Chapter Fourteen
Life Looks Up

Leaving the Carlson farm didn't mean a new life of comfort or a way of normal living for us because we spent the next year back in the basement in Edmonton. But we found we had new neighbors, and we did make a new friend who lived across the street. Much as Duane and I loved one another, we could only talk so much in our grungy cellar, and it was a great relief to our boredom when Patterson built a crystal set for us. It was just a simple radio receiver that was popular in the early days of radio. It needed neither a battery nor a power source and ran on the energy received from radio waves through a long wire antenna.

"Hey, Ed, Duane," he had yelled from his house when he spied us getting home from school. "I got a new radio for my birthday, and I kinda got to thinking that I'll bet you don't have anything to listen to at night, so I put this all together for you."

What a gift that was—practically the first gift we had ever received! Patterson helped us get it hooked up and, while I still don't quite understand how it worked, I know we could magically fine tune it to listen to the radio programs that were popular then. The best signals came after sunset, and since airwaves operate mysteriously, at least to me, the strongest reception came from a radio station in Mexico. We spent many happy hours listening to country music. Thanks to Patterson, two lonely boys in Edmonton, Alberta, whiled away their time listening to XHBIO from Guadalajara over two thousand miles away. I think of him often with gratitude. He was another link to my dream that a better life lay ahead.

We were fifteen years old that last year in Edmonton and were thrilled to discover upon our return from the Carlsons' farm that Dad had made some welcome changes in our living conditions. "I think you'll like what I did for you while you were away," he said, showing us the small room he had constructed for us in the basement. "This will give you a little more privacy." It was very sparse, with plain walls, but it had a raised wooden floor that made our space just a little bit warmer. "But the best part," I whispered to Duane when we heard the cellar door close behind Dad's back when he left us to unpack, "is that now we have a place to get away from Aunt Hildore when she comes down to do the laundry."

The room didn't actually have a door, just an opening where one should have been, but it was a major improvement over being plunked down in the middle of the cellar floor where anyone who came down could see us. In retrospect, I realize how pitiful our lives had been that such a minor change in our circumstances gave us so much pleasure. And it strikes me as being quite odd that Dad never seemed to notice or understand that the conditions we faced daily were frequently dangerous for boys our age, often cruel, and almost always demeaning and an attack on our dignity. Was Dad's blind disregard for our plight deliberate, or were these rather feeble attempts to improve our lot simply his way of coping with Aunt Hildore's contempt for us? Whatever his motives, Dad also had two surprises that would open new horizons for us and would transform our view of our future.

While having our own room seemed little short of a miracle, Dad's other news stunned us. He and Aunt Hildore must have thought it was time for us to branch out on our own, for it was then that he revealed, "Boys, I have wonderful news for you. When your father died, your Uncle Carl, your mother's brother, sold all their china and silverware and furniture, and he put the money away for you. I'm happy to tell you that you have $3,700!" (2013 buying power of approximately $45,000)

"Wow, we're rich!" I exclaimed, not realizing at the time that one day, when I had a home of my own, I would wish I had even a few of their belongings to cherish.

Instead, I said to Duane, "Think of all the wonderful places we can go!" It was wartime, so the stores didn't have a lot of luxury goods for sale, but for Duane and me who had never even had an allowance, this was nirvana indeed. For the first time in our lives, we were going to have fun!

Dad's suggestions were a little more practical, but nevertheless offered interesting possibilities. We accompanied him as we always had on his next monthly visit to the church in Clive. We were anxious to see the Westlings again, for we had missed them, and Dad had hinted that we might learn something new on this visit. After he had preached at Saren Lutheran Church, and as we were on our way to Wetaskiwin for the second worship service of the day, he pointed to an abandoned farm directly across the road from the church.

From the looks of it, the farmhouse hadn't been taken care of for many years; probably no one had lived there since the early days of the Depression. Everything was in a state of total disrepair, and the few outbuildings were leaning so precariously they looked as if the next strong wind would dash them to pieces. Half the windows were broken or missing, and all the structures were surrounded by tall weeds and half-dead trees. The farmstead was the personification of desolation.

"With the money from your parents' estate and with the $2,000 postal savings from your Grandmother Carlson (we wouldn't discover for several years that our Uncle Carl had illegally used those funds,) we could put some money down on that farm and it would be yours," Dad told us. "You could buy a team of horses and some cows and some chickens, and I could buy my eggs from you," he added. "Or," he continued, bringing the second bombshell in as many days, "you could go to live with your sisters."

"Sisters?" we cried in unison. "We have sisters?" It had been so long since we had seen them when we returned from Sweden—and we had been so young then—that we had completely forgotten that they existed. It was almost as if Dad had never mentioned them. Finding out about them opened a new door. "When can we see them?" we wanted to know. Finally, it seemed, we might be like other people with real relatives. We had seen families through their living room windows as we walked home from school and wondered what they were talking about. We had thought about what it would be like to have someone poke us in a teasing moment or double over with laughter at our jokes. Now, we hoped, we would visit our sisters and become part of a family. It was a wonderful vision.

"Yes," Dad explained when our excitement had subsided long enough for him to be heard again, "you boys have two sisters in Nebraska, and you could go and live with them."

We had no idea where Nebraska was, but after seeing the dilapidated farm ("too much like the Carlsons' for me," I thought) and buoyed by the prospect of reuniting with our sisters, we knew that was where we belonged. We hadn't felt so thrilled since our participation in one of the most solemn and significant events of our young lives when we were confirmed in the spring of 1945. We had attended many classes and studied new prayers and hymns in preparation for the service, and it all would have been perfect "if only our father could be with us now," I remarked to Duane. I knew instinctively this would have been a precious moment for him as both pastor and parent. It was obviously important for Dad that we pass this milestone, for he frequently quizzed us on what we were learning, and he took us shopping himself for our new clothes. You would have thought it was his confirmation, the way he puffed his chest and preened as he ordered the salesclerk to be sure the shoulders fit just right. It was certainly the first time anyone had ever suggested that the cuffs on my pants had to break at just the right place on my shoes, but our confirmation ceremony also marked one of the rare times I wouldn't be wearing overalls.

I chuckle when I see how serious and determined the entire class of boys in our photo album looks, but I remember how stiff Duane and I felt in the first suits we had ever owned. The navy serge chafed the insides of our legs, but we knew better than to scratch them or do anything else that might mar the solemnity of the afternoon. It would certainly be a long time before either of us sported a boutonniere in our lapels again, but the most lasting memento of that event is the Bible each boy received that day. I still treasure mine.

A huge flurry of activity ensued as the week for our trip to see our sisters approached, and we frequently overheard Linnea and Miriam discuss which dresses they would pack—"I'm not taking my pink one if you're wearing yours"—and who they would write to while they were gone. It certainly wasn't going to take Duane and me much time to prepare, since what little we owned would fit easily into the old suitcase that had accompanied us on every trip we had ever taken.

Finally, our odyssey to the state of our birth began on July 2, 1946, a fitting time for two young Americans to return to their own country. We had been born in Nebraska, but didn't remember our early years there or almost anything of the time spent in Sweden with our Aunt Huldah. We had always considered Canada our native land, but now I truly realized that I was an American. It was time to go home!

The sun seemed to smile on the six of us as we piled into the Chevy, now a little dented from both age and backcountry roads, filling it with our luggage and a couple of baskets of food. There weren't many places to eat along the highway in the 1940s, and to stop at any that did exist would be time consuming and expensive. Most travelers like us packed picnics to enjoy by the side of the road, and we were always on the lookout for an isolated grove of trees because bathrooms were as scarce as restaurants. The days of fast food were far in the future, and auto trips were frequently a test of endurance, especially in a crowded car.

Aunt Hildore's displeasure at our presence was palpable. She had isolated herself from us for so long that she could hardly bear to have us in the same vehicle. Any attempts we made to converse with the girls were met with glares and reproving looks, so we drove in stony silence. Conversation would have been difficult anyway, because Miriam and Linnea had each insisted on having a window seat. One of us had to sit between them in the back, and the other sat in the middle seat in the front with our feet on the hump in the center of the floor. It was the closest I had been to Aunt Hildore in a long time. I didn't like it much.

Under other circumstances, such proximity to her might have seemed unbearable, but I, for one, was much too nervous about what I would find at the end of the journey to think about it. I had no idea what my sisters would be like, and little of my experience with women had been positive. It was a bit frightening to realize that from now on Duane and I would be on our own, and what we chose to do with our lives would be our own decision. We had slept little the night before, worrying about the future, asking ourselves, "Will they like us? Will they let us live with them? Do you think they'll remember us?"

In some ways, we had been treated like grown men, at least in the responsibilities that had been thrust upon us. At the same time, however, we knew nothing about how to foster personal relationships, and the only adults we had known had been terrible role models for developing family bonds. We had never enjoyed the advantage of caring parents who picked us up after we fell down and advised us what to do next. When I hear parents encouraging their children by saying, "It's okay; you'll do better next time," I realize how deprived we were. We had essentially skipped childhood and the lessons it carried toward adulthood, but here we were being thrust out to face our future with no roadmap to guide us. We were going to be alone, and I was scared to death. For once I had a lot more to fear than Aunt Hildore's wrath or her warm leg jammed up against mine on the crowded seat.

It was a long drive, and the early morning heat that had been so welcome became stifling as the day wore on. It didn't help to relieve it by opening the windows with all the dust that blew in from the highway. Resignedly, we cranked up the windows again, especially when one of the girls complained, "Shut those—the wind is messing up my hair!"

We all sighed with relief when we finally spotted the first sign for Banff and stopped for a two-hour break for lunch and a look around the town. What a beautiful place! The magnificent Banff Springs Hotel, which had been built in 1888, towered above the town, its bulk as imposing as an Edwardian matron and just as unyielding. The Bow River, rushing from its headwaters in the ice fields up north, sparkled in the sunlight as it tumbled by the tourists strolling along its banks. I had never seen the mountains so close before, and the air felt crisp and clean after our stifling drive. "I wonder how it would feel to live in a town like this," I mused. Even the little village of shops seemed different from any I had ever seen before—far from the bustle of Edmonton's cityscape and so much more refined and sophisticated than the streets of Camrose. From store to store, Duane and I wandered in the two hours we had been given to explore on our own before continuing our trip. For once, we had some change in our pockets since Dad had given each of us fifty cents to spend. Perhaps this was a reward for sitting so quietly in the car, or perhaps for once he felt a little sorry for us, for I never remember him giving us spending money before. Or, more likely, he felt Aunt Hildore wouldn't care now that she would be free of us for good.

There were so many souvenirs to choose from—miniature skis and sleds and snowshoes, hand-carved fir trees, and jade bears, triumphant with a catch of salmon caught in their teeth. There were even Christmas shops, carrying only decorations of every description to remind customers each year of their trip to the Canadian Rockies. Striped candy canes, carvings of Canadian Mounties, snowballs and reindeer filled the windows and beckoned shoppers to browse. I still have the plaster moose that I bought that day. It was probably the first luxury purchase I had made since the episode of the Delft doll, and I have treasured it highly all these years. Too soon, we had to pile back into the Chevy and leave that glorious city behind, tucking its memory in a safe place in our imaginations. I noticed the temperature hadn't gotten much cooler once we were crammed in the car, but by that time I was too pleasantly tired to care.

By the end of that uncomfortable ride, we were ready for our stop at the big two-story bed and breakfast where Aunt Hildore bragged Dad had made reservations. Duane and I were exhilarated at the prospect of sleeping in a hotel in which several other families might also be staying. It would be a new experience, and I think it seemed special to the girls as well. Not surprisingly, we didn't remember anything of our return on the liner from Sweden years earlier, and we hadn't been anywhere else since then except when we were sent to a new family. "Thank heavens it won't be anything like that," I whispered to Duane. It was a tantalizing enough thought to help us forget, at least temporarily, our fears of being on our own.

Looking back, I wonder what ever made me think we would sleep in a real bed in a real hotel room like the rest of the family. What made us think we were now going to be treated like normal people? It was probably a good thing that, for the most part, we had learned to cope well with disappointment, for we were rapidly spiraling down for another one.

"Boys," Dad told us, as Aunt Hildore and Linnea and Miriam disappeared into one of the buildings, and he parked the car in an alley, "you two can sleep here. It won't get very cold tonight. Just keep the doors locked and you'll be safe. And if you need to wash up or use the bathroom, you can just go to the gas station across the street."

My hopes plummeted as I faced the reality of our situation, but grim as that treatment might have been, it paled after our nights in the Edmonton cellar. At least here we had separate beds—Duane slept in the front seat and I slept in the back! I might not have been cold, but I sure was cramped, though fortunately, I hadn't achieved my adult size. The sandwiches we had packed in Edmonton had turned soggy and tasted a little off, but we survived as usual. I continued to understand, "If I don't dream now, 'I can make it!' I won't even come close." I was far from formalizing my aspirations for the future, but I had learned at the Carlsons' that with a little imagination and a lot of hard work, I could succeed at nearly anything I attempted. I couldn't afford to let an almost sleepless night and a meager supper dim my vision of a better life, whatever that meant.

On July 4, 1946, we finally reached Axtell, Nebraska, where Dad, our aunt, and the girls stayed with Hildore's mother. In her usual nasty voice, Aunt Hildore was quick to let us know that we wouldn't be staying there. We were too tired to care where we slept, but it warmed our hearts when we overheard Hildore's mother defending us, "Why do you treat these boys like this? Why do you have to be so mean to them?" She was outraged at the way her daughter dealt with us, and for the duration of our short visit, we basked in the awareness of our very own champion. It didn't change anything, but it was comforting to know that someone might actually consider our feelings or care about us after all.

Later that afternoon, Edna Nelson, whom we had scant memories of staying with shortly after we returned from Sweden, drove over with her son Dennis to see everyone. She invited Duane and me to spend that night with her, which was a double treat since it gave us a night away from Aunt Hildore and the prospect of enjoying Edna's very comfortable beds. Edna even filled our plates twice!

This affectionate attention helped mitigate the disappointment we had felt upon learning that no one was quite sure how to contact our sisters once we reached the United States, and I don't believe Dad had really tried. If one knew the city a person lived in, it was possible to find him in a telephone book listing or through the information service, but otherwise it was a daunting task. The instant response of the Internet was yet to come. Exasperated at our constant stream of questions about when we would meet Ruth and Alice, Aunt Hildore had snapped, "Never mind about them. We don't know where they are. We only want to get you to school and then you can find them—that is, if they want to see you," she had added spitefully.

After that we had lapsed into morose silence and resolved not to mention them again in her hearing. That last comment bothered me, making me realize that either our sisters didn't care about re-connecting with us or that they had no idea how to find us. As it turned out, they were initially leery of re-establishing a relationship with us, but once we met them and they realized that we were safely independent of them at our school, they were happy to see us. When we learned more about their lives, we understood they hadn't had much more opportunity than us to develop family feelings or understand the value of those ties. In the meantime, we had lots of adjustments to make ourselves.

On our second morning in Nebraska, Dad came out to Edna's farm to take us to Alfreda Benson's house in Wahoo, where we would later attend Luther Academy. He had never met Mrs. Benson, nor did he make any attempt to do so that day. It was just another example of his assumptions that we could be moved from place to place like pawns on a chessboard. We had arrived in the land of the free, but we wouldn't experience our first taste of real freedom for some time to come.

It was about a three-hour drive before Dad stopped his Chevy in front of Mrs. Benson's home. "Just take your things into the house, boys," he instructed us. "I'll wait out here until you come back so we can say our good-byes."

It didn't take us long, for all we had was one blanket each and the old familiar suitcase that contained all our possessions. In less than five minutes we returned, and, with a hasty pat on the back, he got into his car and started to drive off. We stood there in total disbelief that his good-byes had been so brief, and we could feel the hot wind blowing our tears away. Once again we were two abandoned orphans, completely alone in the world. Just as the car began to disappear, to our great delight we saw it come back toward us, easing up in front of the house where we were standing, and slowly approaching our dejected figures.

"He's come back to get us!" I exclaimed. I was crying my eyes out, and through the blur I thought he was waving. But no, Dad simply rolled down the window, and leaning slightly toward us, he admonished, "Boys, be careful how you live; you might be the only Bible some people ever read."

With that he again drove off, and I only saw him twice more in my life. It's sad to think how often he left us to the ill treatment of strangers, but for our part we never did anything to disappoint him.

Chapter Fifteen
Discovering America

It really never occurred to Dad how difficult it was for Duane and me to endure these constant upheavals or how we suffered emotionally and mentally without a permanent home.

Fortunately for us, Mrs. Benson was one of the kinder strangers in our extraordinary odyssey of growing up, and living with her eased our journey to becoming full-fledged Americans. Our living quarters were below conventional standards, for we had only a dirt floor in our basement bedroom, but this time we didn't mind. Showing us a small rug by the side of our bed, our landlady cautioned us, "Mind you, boys, wipe your feet before you get into that bed. I don't want to see any footprints on those sheets!" Mrs. Benson's words might have seemed to carry an edge, but I knew from her tone of voice that she really meant, "I'm giving you the best I have, and I hope you'll do all right down here." Of course, she could have no idea to what we had become accustomed, or how the warmth of her expression endeared her to us.

As we got to know her better, we developed a special affection for Mrs. Benson, and later, when we were in school in Wahoo, we often visited her to see if she needed any help. We learned one time when we were on our way to shovel her sidewalk that she also had a sense of humor.

Always a feisty lady whose energy belied her years—she seemed old to us, but was probably in her seventies then—she had started to clear her path of the several inches of snow that had fallen the night before. Her cheeks were chapped from the ever present cold and the gray curls straying from her brightly knitted cap were blowing in the wind, but her blue eyes snapped with pleasure as she spied us.

"Duane, Ed," she called to us. "How good to see you! It's been a while. I missed seeing you at church yesterday!"

"Oh, we went to vespers," we answered."Where were you sitting?" she asked.

"Oh," Duane replied, almost too quickly for complete honesty, "we were up in the balcony." "Really?" she responded, with a twinkle in her eye and a roguish smile on her lips. "Really?" she repeated. "We always have vespers in the basement!"

We were caught! In all sincerity, it was the only time we ever missed a Sunday service in our years at school, and it escapes me how we dodged the rest of her questions. I suppose we must have stammered some explanation in our confusion, but I know it taught us a valuable lesson. When I remember that moment, I laugh heartily at our predicament and realize how discomfited we felt at being caught out in a lie. I appreciate how much Mrs. Benson enjoyed her amusement at our expense. She must have been a lonely old woman, and we certainly brightened that day for her.

Our time was our own while we stayed at Mrs. Benson's, and we used it to get to know the town. "You hungry?" I would ask Duane. "Yup," he'd nod. We had found a restaurant down by a truck stop where we could get cheap, hearty food, and we paid for our meals with money we earned cleaning windows, raking leaves, and changing screens and storm windows for people who needed help fixing up their houses at the end of summer. It was only late August, but fall comes early in that part of the country, and winter is never far behind. "Sure, boys, I could use a hand," the older residents would assure us. "And when you're done, maybe you'd like a cup of cocoa.""I think they like the company as much as they need the help," I would remark to Duane. We were learning that people might enjoy us for ourselves and not just for what we could do for them.

Our work routines in Camrose had prepared us to take care of ourselves, but we now enjoyed one major difference in Wahoo. We had money in our pockets, and we were our own bosses. When we weren't already working, we would hang around the local gas station, washing the car windows as drivers waited for the attendant to fill their tanks and listening to the conversations around us. It was a great way to pick up information or other available work, and it was a good way to meet some of the locals. It was also a way to learn how other guys our age lived, since our life experience was pretty limited when it came to social life.

For the first time we discovered that Dad's rules of behavior were a bit stricter than the average, and it was easily the first time that we had the opportunity to question them. For the most part, Dad's principles won out, but it was also the first time we ever understood what fun it was to relax.

"Let's see what's going on in town," I might suggest. There was always a sense of expectancy in the air in the long evenings of summer, and to our unsophisticated minds there seemed to be an endless list of possibilities. Postwar ebullience pervaded the population. Girls in brightly colored skirts flirted coyly with boys languishing in tight little groups on the corner, and everyone seemed ready for fun. It was only a year since the end of the war, and people still loved to celebrate the end of rationing and shortages.

"Hey," one of the guys would offer, "we're going out to get drunk tonight— you want to join us?"

Duane and I were so naive that we had no idea how to answer such an invitation. We would walk away and huddle together, whispering, "What do you think Dad would say?" "I don't think he'd like it," the answer would come. Then, trying to add a little swagger to our steps, we would stroll back to the group and respond, "Maybe some other time."

Another would ask, "Want a smoke?" Again we would whisper, "What do you think Dad would say?" Once again we would refuse the offer. We were anomalies among the young men in the town. A cigarette hanging from the corner of a young man's mouth was as much a part of the uniform of the day as a plaid shirt and jeans. For a number of reasons, we never smoked or drank. Our church and our uncle were great influences on us in that regard— we still measured much of our behavior against Dad's standards—but we never let on that we had yet to try cigarettes or alcohol. It was a good thing, anyway, since either one would have caused a great strain on our finances.

After we had been with Mrs. Benson for ten days, Edna called to see if either Duane or I would like to help out on her farm. She had also learned that her cousin, Mildred Juergens, could use an extra hand where she farmed near Beaver City, so I went to the Juergens family while Duane worked on the Nelson farm. We spent the last six weeks of the summer at our respective jobs.

Most days brought more of the same hard work I had gotten used to at the Carlsons' farm. The mornings started before the nights had drawn to a close, and, like a true farmer, I was up even before dawn. The alarm rang at four in the morning, and the daily chores were always finished before breakfast. After I had eaten, Mr. Juergens would assign whatever odd jobs he wanted me to do, and I would be out in the fields or the barns for the rest of the day.

Only one task stands out in my mind. It was just an ordinary morning when Mr. Juergens brought out the corn knife, a square tool with a serrated edge like a saw. "I want you to go out and cut the cockleburs that are growing by the road," he told me. It was important to get rid of them because otherwise they would seed themselves and strangle the crops in the adjacent fields. In addition to that, their prickly seed husks stuck to the trousers of anyone working near them and got tangled in the farm dog's fur. (It was burrs that led to the invention of Velcro.) "But watch out," the farmer added, "the ditches are full of snakes."

Now not much frightens me, but there is one thing that terrifies me, and that is snakes. These weren't just your garden-variety garter snakes, they were mean and dangerous rattlesnakes that attacked swiftly and fatally. I learned to cut quickly and cleanly before I could awaken the sleeping rattlers and managed to escape harm. For that I was paid one dollar a day. I soon found a good way to use that money.

At that time, Beaver City epitomized rural communities all over the American plains, and with a population of less than seven hundred souls and an area only about one square mile, the word *city* was a misnomer after Edmonton. However, it was the seat of Furnas County and the home of a busy co-op where the community came alive each Saturday night.

The country might have been on the cusp of a new prosperity, but in a town like Beaver City in the heart of an agricultural area, there wasn't much employment for returning soldiers, especially those who were injured or maimed. Even many of the able-bodied still had to endure hard times. I just couldn't stand to see men aimlessly milling around with hungry looks on their faces, hoping for a handout. I guess I recognized that they didn't have any hope for the future. They didn't share the feeling I still harbored from my days in the basement when I used to think, "If I don't dream now, 'I can make it!' I won't even come close." As I said earlier, I still didn't have a clear vision of what I wanted, but I was sure that one day I could expect a happier and more successful life.

I was walking down Main Street and wondering how I would spend the rest of the evening one Saturday when a man came up to me, saying, "I'm so hungry; could you spare a dollar so I can get something to eat?" I wanted to help him, but I had overheard conversations between Juergens and his neighbors about panhandlers looking for handouts so they could buy liquor. Not wanting to start him on that slippery slope, I took his arm and led him to the City Café.

When we walked in, the hostess approached us and asked, "Table for two, sir?" I responded, "No, just for this man. He's hungry, so would you please take his order and put your tip on the bill. I'll wait here until you bring me the check when he's finished." The bill came to three dollars including the tip. I paid it and left. I still had four dollars left and felt rich. I wonder now what the waitress thought of me, the scraggly young man who bought dinners for strangers, since I did this a few more times during my summer in Beaver City. Where I had learned about tipping, I'm still not sure.

"Imagine," I would think later, she called me 'sir'!" Maybe I was already learning about the possibility of better times. I savored this sign of respect which was a far cry from the verbal abuse I was used to receiving. I was learning that having a little money in my pocket could engender feelings of power and importance, and I probably preened a bit. But I was also enjoying the truth of one of Dad's favorite sayings, "Boys, the true measure of a man is how he treats someone who can do him absolutely no good." I've never forgotten that.

As summer drew to a close, I realized how much I missed Duane, and I was more than ready to leave Beaver City. My brother and I planned to stay with the Nelsons until school started, so Edna and Dennis came to pick me up at the Juergens' farm. What a reunion Duane and I enjoyed, and with the two of us splitting the chores at the Nelsons, we relaxed on the first vacation of our lives. We slept a little later than usual and spent some of our newly earned money to purchase the few supplies and basic necessities we knew we needed for school.

Those final days passed quickly before it was time for Edna and Dennis to drive us to our dorm in Wahoo. The town's name comes from an Indian word meaning "burning bush," and seemed an apt location for two boys who had been raised with a strict interpretation of the Bible. Like us, the town had a strong Scandinavian background—it had been founded in 1870 by a group of settlers who hoped this area would become one of the richest farming regions in the state.

Thanks to the $3,700 bequest from the sale of our parents' possessions, which would cover some of our expenses, we had been accepted at Luther Academy, a four-year high school that also offered an additional two years of college and had a boarding facility where we could live. The academy had been founded thirteen years after the town by a Swedish immigrant who had graduated from Augustana College in Rock Island, Illinois, where my parents had studied. Dad thought highly of it since it was a Lutheran establishment where we would keep close to church teachings and customs. Its main building had been dedicated on November 10, 1883, exactly four hundred years after the birth of Martin Luther.

Sometimes, I wonder if Dad harbored hopes that one of us would follow in the footsteps that he and our father had forged, but he never said so. He did write something about me becoming a minister in a prayer book he once gave me, but he never actually put it into spoken words. However, I will be forever grateful for the deep faith that he instilled in Duane and me which has always been an integral part of my life. Night after night without fail, when we lived in Edmonton, he would come downstairs to hear our prayers, and I can still hear the echo of our voices as we recited the simple words in Swedish that began "God forgive my sins" and ended "fill my heart with happiness." Then he would turn out the light and leave us in the darkness.

Although the irony of our situation didn't occur to me until later—that insistence that Duane and I kneel down in prayer before going to sleep on one bed in a damp basement—I can still trace the early roots of my deep faith in God to those nightly rituals. Dad certainly had a strange way of expressing his feelings for "my brother's boys" as he frequently called us, but whatever conclusions I or others may draw about his motives, I know that today I am grateful to Dad for my spiritual values.

He always started his occasional letters to us with a scriptural reference, his favorite being, "the Lord is my shepherd, I shall not want" from Psalm twenty-three. He also wrote that in a hymnal he gave me in which he inscribed the words "with love and prayer from Dad, Mom and Mir to our dear Edwin, Edmonton, Alberta, September 11, 1951." By then, Linnea had married and moved away.

One phrase in particular from one of his letters sticks in my mind: "We know that everything works together for good for them that love God." Now I find this another example of his pietism, as if he was trying to prove to himself that he was taking an active role in raising "my brother's boys."

Chapter Sixteen
Academic Doldrums

When I awoke on the first morning of classes at Luther Academy, I could barely keep my hands from shaking with trepidation. Here I was, feeling and looking like a country farm boy, and I knew I was poised on the threshold of a new life. I trembled at the thought of what lay before me.

As Duane and I covered the short distance from our dormitory to the handsome brick building called Old Main, I looked at the other young men gathered around the bottom steps that led to the front door and was dismayed at what I observed. Not one student resembled Duane or me. It wasn't that some were tall, and we were still short, or that most were well barbered, and we looked raked by a scythe. It wasn't even that their neatly pressed slacks and shirts made our jeans and army surplus jackets look so tacky. It was the way they stood, so sleek and sure of themselves. I was sorry no one had suggested that we save some of our pay to buy new clothes when we had outgrown our confirmation suits, but I recognized a much greater difference. We felt out of our depth because we were. Those kids were comfortable in their own skin, and we felt constrained by ours.

Duane and I had rarely associated with people who lived much above the subsistence level, and we had no notion of what constituted actual wealth. We tended to attach a label of rich folks to almost anyone who was smartly dressed or appeared better off than we were. Since almost everyone did, we thought that some people were rich even if they had middle class incomes. That's how we felt about the boys and girls milling about the lawn. Strangely enough, we learned later that some of our classmates made the same mistake about us. They thought we came from a rich, eccentric family—eccentric because we wore long work pants, usually denim, and they wore worsted wools or finer cottons—and rich because we came all the way from Canada!

It would be a long time before we learned that, however, and in the meantime, the knowledge that we looked down at the heels increased our general feelings of inadequacy.

That first day, we moved into our dormitory, and though the furnishings might have seemed almost monastic to the other boys on the hall, to us they appeared substantial. "Okay, Duane," I suggested when I saw the bunks, a luxury for us, "let's shoot for who gets the upper and who sleeps below. We can take turns then." I remember thinking with elation that we would no longer have to sleep in basements.

A desk and two chairs filled the small space, and there was a closet (although we had few clothes to fill it) in one corner opposite the door. We hardly noticed the scratches on the floors or the marks on the walls where former occupants had shoved the beds or hung pictures of their families. This was our own room with a door we could shut and a window we could open. Best of all, we even had a radio, the first we had ever personally owned apart from the crystal set Patterson had made for us. When Edna Nelson had driven us to Minden, a town near Axtell, to shop for a few school supplies, to our great delight we had found a radio we could afford. It didn't matter to us that it was secondhand and had a cracked case. It worked, and it was ours.

One incident occurred early in our first semester at Luther to reinforce what we recognized as the disparity of disposable income between us and much of the student body. This was reflected most noticeably in the extent of our respective wardrobes. A bunch of boys were hanging around after chapel, which was compulsory every day, when one of them suggested, "Hey, guys, who wants to 'chute'?"

There was a rather odd fire escape on the third floor outside the chapel that had been constructed to make evacuation of the building as speedy as possible in an emergency. Students had discovered it provided an entertaining way to amuse themselves after the long prayers and readings and announcements. Unlike the traditional iron grills and ladders or steep stairs that characterized most fire escapes, this was really a slide that provided a most satisfying ride to the bottom. We called the procedure 'chuting.'

On this particular day, we threw our shoes down first, as we were accustomed to, but unbeknownst to us, the president of the school, Mr. Lauerson, hid near the bottom and collected them all before the first boy descended. When we got to the ground, all our shoes had disappeared! There was just enough time before class for everyone to get back to the dormitories to get another pair before the first bell rang. That was okay for the other students, but Duane and I had only one pair of shoes each, and so we had to appear at class with only socks on our feet. Professor Iverne Dowie was blind and couldn't see our lack of shoes. However, at class that afternoon when we had to write on the blackboard, another teacher glimpsed our stockinged feet and thought we were trying to be smart-alecks. When we confessed our predicament, however, she kindly went to the president and got our shoes back. That effectively ended our adventures on the fire escape.

Attending Luther was our first experience of associating regularly with boys who enjoyed the easygoing complacency that comes from growing up in a home where a father leaves in the morning to earn a comfortable salary and returns every night to read his paper. We didn't know about mothers who shopped with their children for new clothes before school started, and we had only a vague recollection of our friend Johnny Allen Martin's tears being kissed away by his mother after he had fallen from the swing at Grandahl's. The concept of a stable family life functioning on the basis of love and respect was as foreign to us as a father who played ball with his sons or a mother who taught her daughters to dance. Gazing around that first day, we suffered genuine pangs of inferiority that made us both yearn for the first week to be over.

It would be many years before I realized how many of my friends considered me good-looking or how my natural congeniality attracted people. I was learning slowly about the power of determination and perseverance to overcome obstacles, but I didn't yet have much confidence in my own abilities. I was too used to being called names and treated like an outcast. I just had to remind myself that we needed more education if we had any expectations of amounting to anything. We were raw material that needed shaping to form a finished product, and I knew this school was an excellent place to start. I recognized that this was a good place to nurture my dream of success.

When we finally settled in to our first classes, it was clear our teachers had no idea how far behind we were. Even though we had gone to school regularly during the last year in Edmonton, we needed a lot of catching up. No one realized we lacked the most basic skills, since the administration hadn't required an entrance examination, and we didn't have a transcript detailing our scant achievements. I still thought mainly in Swedish, and my spelling and writing were atrocious. It would take hours of studying and more than a little expert bluffing if we were to avoid being laughingstocks in most of our subjects. Attending Luther Academy was going to be much different from going to class in the one room schools of Alberta and not just because we missed the cozy rooms and pot-bellied stoves.

I, for one, felt extremely apprehensive about keeping up, and I knew that our biggest obstacle lay in the fact that we had never learned to apply ourselves to academics. No parent had checked up on our homework or held out the promise of a new game if we won the spelling bee or brought home a good report card, and nobody had cared if we had a star at the top of our composition or if we blotted our papers with ink from our fountain pens.

Most of the time I had been too tired to do my homework, and up until now it hadn't seemed important. As I recall, at some point I had developed beautiful penmanship, and now I prided myself more on the appearance of my schoolwork than on its content. Unfortunately, no one ever noticed that I was a natural draftsman, and I only developed those skills for my own personal satisfaction. (I can still draw to scale the basement of the house in Edmonton and the attic room we occupied at the Carlsons' farm.)

Our classes were small, with an average of about fifteen students in each, so I'm not sure why we didn't achieve greater academic success at Luther. Our life experiences had attuned us to hard work, but it had always been of a physical nature. We'd never been given the chance to pursue the intellectual outlets that had marked our mother's and father's interests, and it wasn't until I was older that I discovered the true joys of reading. I have a postcard my father sent to Dad when he was packing to attend college in Rockford in which he mentions the books he was sending. At the end of the note a postscript says simply, "Also Cicero." I am embarrassed now to think how many years it was before I realized he was referring to the ancient Roman philosopher and statesman and not a friend with an unusual name.

Having to contend with this abysmal background, our teachers tired of hearing us stumble over the answers when they called on us, and by the end of the first semester we were barely encouraged to participate in class. We weren't exactly thrown to the wolves, but our teachers didn't reach out to us either. Soon, we gave up struggling with our homework and assignments and fell further and further behind. We never spoke up in class—we just attended—and when our teachers noticed our shoddy work, they started to skip over us in favor of more alert students.

Tutoring was nonexistent at the academy, but even if it had been available, we couldn't have afforded to pay for additional help, and there weren't any study halls where we might have been forced to exercise our brains. As a result, we sat there, ignored, until we were promoted to the next grade, regardless of our lack of preparation.

Duane and I drifted during our four years there, and for the first time in my life I lost sight of the dream that I could make a better life for myself. I sometimes wonder if all our teachers knew our sad story and just assumed that all we could contribute was our presence. When they got together at the end of the day in the faculty lounge, did they just shake their heads and sigh, "Can these really be Pastor Vikman's sons?"

I remember one friend, Phil Youngquist, who helped us when he could, but since our report cards were sent to Dad in Edmonton, we had no idea if his assistance was effective. We didn't realize at the time how strange it was that Dad made no comments on our grades, and we didn't think to ask him. Perhaps he thought his only responsibility for our education was in enrolling us at the academy.

We had almost no contact either with him or with Aunt Hildore during our time at Luther. I remember one startling letter in which Dad enclosed ten dollars for books, with a promise of another note to come from Mom. Since it was almost impossible to detect even a hint of warmth or feeling in anything he wrote, this magnanimous gift surprised us in its generosity.

Questions about Dad recur over and over again in my thoughts, even at eighty-two years of age. I still can't help asking myself, "Did Dad find expressing his emotions embarrassing, and was he afraid to display affection, or did his behavior simply reflect an empty sense of obligation?" How hard it is to be so unsure.

Chapter Seventeen
Sister Search

Although we had come to the States to find our sisters, we discovered soon after we started school that, just as time hadn't stood still for us, the years had brought many changes for them as well. Once our uncle had reminded us about them, little snippets of memory from our visit to Holdrege after our return from Sweden flashed through my head. From the deep recesses of my brain, I recaptured an image of grown-up girls affectionately hugging us, probably the last time a relative had touched us with love. I had felt a bit in awe of those tall young ladies, especially Ruth, who by then was almost on the brink of womanhood; Alice was already a budding teenager. Now when Duane or I mentioned them by name, that was how I pictured them.

On a day in late October, Pastor A. Eugene Larson, whom we had met shortly after we arrived at Luther Academy, looked us up to tell us wonderful news. "Ed and Duane," he said, not realizing how much Duane liked being addressed first, "I've been doing a little research on your behalf, and I think I know where to find your sisters. If I'm right, I'm pretty sure I'm acquainted with one of their in-laws. We can take a drive to Omaha to see what we can find out about them." "In-laws?" I questioned? "You mean they're married?" I grinned at Duane. "I guess they've gotten older, too!"

A few Saturdays later, we piled into the pastor's car and headed to the city, just about forty minutes away. It's impossible to describe how excited we were. We'd been in Nebraska since July, but we were finally going to find our sisters. We thought we were going to see them that day, despite the fact that Pastor Larson had warned us of his uncertainty of their actual whereabouts. Our anticipation deafened us to his words of caution.

We knew by now from Pastor Larson that both sisters had gotten married in a double wedding, but we still didn't know why they had apparently moved from Holdrege to Omaha. It wasn't really a great distance, but the people we had known had mostly stayed where they had grown up, unless they had become orphans like us or suffered some other traumatic event. We just assumed that Ruth and Alice had now made Omaha their permanent home. What did we know about people whose new jobs took them to other cities or careers that influenced where you might choose to live? Our moves had been directed by situations beyond our control and, all too frequently, by people who cared little about what became of us or where we were as long as it suited their convenience.

Thinking of the new directions of my sisters' lives made me consider for the first time that I had the option to choose my own future. I was beginning to expand my dreams, but I recognized that nothing would happen without a mighty effort on my part. "But such thinking," I whispered to myself, "is just too scary to handle right now." It was enough to anticipate the reunion with our sisters. We were sure we were just hours away from that meeting.

Though the trip was short, poor Pastor Larson was quite frazzled by the time we got to the Johnson home where Ruth's in-laws lived. We kept asking him for information he couldn't supply, and unlike the two taciturn teenagers he was accustomed to, we peppered him with question after question. "What do they look like? Do you think they'll remember us? Do you think they'll like us?" Those were the same questions we had entertained on our way to Nebraska when we were first getting used to the idea of having sisters. Now, our minds refused to comprehend that we might not see them on this trip since we still had no information about where they and their husbands were living.

Pastor Larson appeared relieved to stem the flow of questions when he finally pulled up to the Johnson's house, remarking, "I think we're here, boys. Now just let me talk to Mrs. Johnson first, and I'll see what I can find out about your sisters." He needn't have worried. As we sat in the car after he parked on Ida Street, we were reduced to our usual uncommunicative selves. We nervously watched him climb the front steps and ring the doorbell. After what seemed an interminable length of time, we saw the front door open and a middle aged woman greeted him. Finally he beckoned to us, so we slowly got out of the car and walked up to join him.

We were tongue tied in front of this stranger, but Pastor Larson expected to do most of the talking, and we were glad to let him. At first we weren't sure who was who as we entered the house. We knew we had only two sisters, but there saying hello to us was an older woman named Sarah—we had no idea who she was—and three younger women, all of whom looked too old to be our sisters. "I guess we forgot," I said to Duane that night when we had gotten back to Luther Academy, "that Ruth and Alice have grown older just like we have."

Since it was a Saturday, everyone was at home, and we were soon introduced to all the Johnsons—Dorothy, who we later learned worked for Mobil Oil, and Gladys, who also had a good job. They supported their mother and sister, Grace, who had had polio. The illness had affected her nervous system, but it hadn't prevented her from developing an incredible talent for baking, as we soon discovered. She had concocted the gooiest chocolate cake we had ever tasted—we were delighted when she insisted we take some back with us—and she also offered us each a second tall glass of milk. We devoured every drop of it and didn't leave a cake crumb on our plates.

I remember I was too embarrassed to ask questions about our sisters, but when we had finished eating, Mrs. Johnson finally brought out some newspapers, saying, "I guess you'd like to see your sisters' wedding pictures."

"Are these our sisters?" I gasped as I gazed at the two brides. "Gosh, they sure are pretty," I breathed in awe. But then the rest of the words in the article sank in. As I read on, I learned that Ruth and her husband, Raymond, had honeymooned in Estes Park, Colorado, while Alice and her new spouse, Einar Christianson, now lived in Worcester, Massachusetts. Ruth and Raymond had moved to Milwaukee, Wisconsin, which seemed an impossible distance to us.

"Oh, Duane," I cried abjectly, "they're not here! We're not going to see them today!" Fortunately for us, we had no idea how much time would elapse before we would at long last reunite with either of them. I think the disappointment of knowing that would have been difficult to bear that day.

We left a little while later, but we visited the Johnsons whenever we could while we were in Wahoo, especially in the spring and fall when they welcomed our offers to winterize their windows with storms or add screens in warmer weather. On one of our visits, we had met Mr. Johnson, who had lost his hands to frostbite during a bitterly cold winter. Now, there were lots of tasks he could no longer accomplish, and we counted it a fair exchange to help get their home ready for the coming season in exchange for enjoying Grace's confections. Observing the sisters and their mother collaborate in sustaining their two disabled relatives was an important lesson for Duane and me. We were gaining first hand insights into the dynamics of family values and relationships that had eluded us until then.

It was difficult to accept that our quest to meet our sisters was temporarily stymied, but we tried to get as much information as possible about them since we had last been together. We were learning that the patterns of their lives had followed quite divergent paths from ours, although they, too, had suffered upheaval and unpleasant change. We found out that our Grandmother Carlson had died in 1938, and by then our grandfather, at seventy-eight years of age, had become quite frail and could no longer support our sisters. As a result, Ruth and Alice were separated. Ruth was sent to live with a much older couple named Ketchum in Omaha—how she must have envied the other girls she met there who had sisters or close friends who could share her adolescent dreams. This new family was affectionate and kind to her, but, like our grandparents, they had not had any young women in their home for many years, and modern teenagers baffled them. Nevertheless, Ruth developed a fond relationship with them and always called him Daddy Ketchum. I've never learned whether she was expected to act as a general housekeeper for them as they grew older, but I know she fared much better than her younger sister.

Alice, who was about eleven at the time, had to live with our mother's brother, Carl Carlson. He was no nicer to her than he ever was to us, since, like many unhappy individuals, he transferred the blame for his misfortunes to his nearest victim. He frequently threatened to place her in an orphanage if her behavior didn't meet his expectations. How reminiscent of what he had wanted to do with us!

Strangely enough, she told us in later years with tears in her eyes, Carl's son, Phillip, was always kind to her, and they were more like brother and sister than cousins. His consideration, however, never extended as far as defending her against his father's demands, and Aunt Elizabeth, Uncle Carl's wife, wasn't any more effective in that regard. One of Alice's greatest humiliations while she lived with Uncle Carl, she once confided to my wife, was his insistence that commercial sanitary protection was much too expensive and old cloths would just have to do. His malice could be very creative.

Until we met our sisters, we had only the newspaper clipping Mrs. Johnson had offered to us that first afternoon in Omaha, but that slip of newsprint was a vital connection to our past. When I looked at the portraits of the two women gazing solemnly into the future from the pages of the paper, their faces glowing like the satin of their gowns, I could only pray we would all be reunited in the near future. Until that transpired a few years later, letters had to suffice as our sole connection.

Almost nobody but the wealthy traveled by air in the late 1940s, so Duane and I couldn't believe our eyes when we tore open a letter from Ruth one day in November 1949 to find plane tickets neatly folded into the pages covered with her deep blue script. We received so few letters that we rarely visited the mail room except when one of our friends invited us to share a care package they were expecting from home. On that late fall day, the sight of the pale yellow envelope that signaled a letter from Ruth raised the usual goose bumps of pleasure for both of us, but our delight escalated as we scanned the lines. To our astonishment, she and Raymond were inviting us to visit them for Christmas in Milwaukee! At long last, we would finally meet one of our sisters, and we would have a real Christmas with our own family— my dream was coming true, and our lives had new meaning. In the weeks before our trip, I practically shredded those precious cardboard tickets as I read and reread the magical words on the colorful sleeve that proclaimed "Braniff Airways, Great Lakes to the Gulf." The romance that I cultivated with automobiles and model trains when I grew older never quite extended to airplanes, but those words promised a trip no flying carpet could equal.

Our visit delivered much more than we ever could have envisioned, as we enjoyed trips to the Milwaukee County Zoo, sampled German brats, and even admired the Roman Catholic Basilica of St. Josaphat, still considered one of the city's most beautiful landmarks. All that paled, however, in comparison to the welcome we received and the love and admiration we basked in for the first time in our lives. Ruth said she wanted to do for us what we had missed during our deprived and motherless childhood. She made special meals—we had our own bedroom—she laughed at our jokes—we exulted in our role of indulgent uncles as we played on the floor with her little boys, Jeff and Bob. It seemed that at least one of my dreams had materialized. We had a family at last, a sense that was enhanced the following spring with the news that Alice and her husband had moved to Des Moines, Iowa. They would be living even closer than Ruth, and we discovered we would be able to hitchhike there quite easily to see them.

Chapter Eighteen
Getting By

Our semi-nomadic life had taught us lessons of ingenuity and flexibility, two qualities that we were called on to practice often when we got to Luther Academy. Although many of the students lived too far away to go home every day, especially during the long winters when the days are short and dark falls early, everyone left school for the weekends, and the dining hall was closed on Saturdays and Sundays. It didn't seem to occur to the headmaster or any of our teachers that Duane and I were stuck at school every Saturday and Sunday with no prospect of meals except for what we might scrounge for ourselves.

Luckily, the food gods had an eye out for us, for they saw to it that Mr. Olson, the janitor, noticed our plight. He would frequently come over from his house in Wahoo to check the campus on Saturdays and took pity on us when he discovered we stayed in the dormitory all weekend with nowhere to get anything to eat. "Just meet me at the back of the dining hall," he told me one day, "and I'll have some bread for you." We figured he either felt sorry for us or wanted to make sure he didn't find us passed out from starvation on Monday morning.

From then on, a visit to the cafeteria became part of our weekend routine, although two pieces of bread wouldn't have satisfied us if we hadn't been able to augment them with eggs or other food we could barter or forage. We had made an arrangement at local farms near the academy to clean the chicken coops each Saturday. In return for this and other chores, we would be paid in cracked eggs.

Back at the academy, we would sneak into the girls' ground floor dormitory where we would fry the eggs on the irons. How in the world we ever thought of that is a mystery because even the poorest homes we had lived in had some kind of stove. Sometimes our resourcefulness was really put to work in high gear. We would eat the eggs with the two pieces of bread and called them gypsy sandwiches. They were delicious, or so we thought, and they certainly filled our growling stomachs. We never tried too hard to get those irons clean, and I wonder how the girls reacted if they noticed dried yolk on them. We just wiped them off the best we could if we thought about it at all.

Since pastors' sons received special tuition rates, we were also given twenty-five cents (roughly three dollars in 2013) each weekend, and that enabled us to get a sandwich or a small pie at the local grocery. It didn't bring much satisfaction to our voracious appetites, so if we were to survive on our own (since all the money we had inherited went toward our tuition and board) Duane and I were constantly on the lookout for odd jobs to earn some cash.

A great opportunity came along when Professor Dowie hired us to wax and polish his car for the lordly sum of five dollars. We worked diligently, but we soon discovered that the professor's blindness didn't always hamper his powers of observation. He had bought a new Ford to impress his lady friend and she, of course, had to drive it. She insisted it be kept as glossy as when it had left the showroom floor. One entire afternoon, we sweated as we labored with a can of Blue Coral hard paste polish and brought the finish to a mirror-bright patina. We knew if we did a good job Professor Dowie might pass the word to the rest of the faculty that the Vikman boys give good value for the money. We were feeling prosperous and satisfied with our work when we presented the car to him for his inspection.

Professor Dowie ran his hand carefully over the whole body of the automobile, and with a smile on his face announced, "You missed this spot, boys." We applied a little more wax and another fifteen minutes of muscle and went back to our dormitory five dollars richer. We could anticipate a hearty repast that weekend.

It probably looked as if we were just idling around town, but in actuality we always had an eye on the help wanted fliers in store windows to help fill our wallets. In fact, if we had expended as much effort on our schoolwork as we did on earning money, we might have been valedictorians! No job was too menial if it meant payment in return, and after all the work we had put in at the farms over the years, we were strong enough to tackle almost anything that came our way. Local businessmen frequently called the school when work was available, and Duane and I were always available. And we took virtually any job that was offered.

That, for example, explains how we became grave diggers. Although ministers and politicians alike may extol honest work of every stripe, there has always been a stigma attached to working in a cemetery and thus there are usually job openings in that field. Cemetery employment ranks among the least palatable of blue-collar jobs, maybe because it is connected to the widespread fear of death. However, whenever we had the chance, Duane and I dug graves. We earned five dollars for each one, and we thought we were millionaires. Somebody once told me that being buried alive or fear of the dark could frighten potential grave diggers, but since we had lived in a dark hole for much of our youth, we didn't share that phobia. We dug.

We learned that hanging around the rail yards also offered potential for getting work, and the pay wasn't bad. We unloaded coal cars and we learned how to man jacks at the new grain elevator being built in Wahoo. We earned one dollar and a quarter per hour and learned that even a small sum, judiciously set aside, could amount to substantial savings. We never forgot that life lesson.

Another source of income turned up when the administrators of Luther Academy decided to build a football field in 1949. Football mania had gripped America since the nineteenth century, but the sport's popularity had waned during the Depression when fielding a team became too expensive for most school districts; football, in fact, largely disappeared during World War II. Now in the new prosperity and euphoria of the postwar era, this great American sport was making a comeback.

Working on the new athletic grounds was a heaven-sent opportunity for Duane and me to add to our coffers, and it offered an exciting prospect as well—a local philanthropist had donated an army surplus dump truck to transport loads of manure from nearby farms to the new field. "Would you guys like to learn how to drive a big rig?" the foreman asked us. How could we ever pass up such an exciting chance? "Imagine," I thought out loud with stars in my eyes at the thought of being at the wheel of this behemoth, "it couldn't be any harder than handling a tractor." I soon learned it was a different skill—and much more fun. It was also an invaluable experience because over the years I drove an assortment of large trucks in a variety of jobs before I settled on my final career, and during my last year at Luther I added another skill when I worked for a man who owned a moving company. "How would you guys like to learn how to drive these trucks?" he asked Duane and me when we met him. "I need someone I can teach to lift and move furniture."

Duane and I became quite expert not only at hoisting breakfronts and appliances, but also at reassuring nervous homeowners that their valuables would arrive safely at their new homes. "Oh, we understand, Ma'am," Duane or I would hasten to say when someone blurted, "young man, you be careful. That belonged to my grandmother."

In this job, we became well acquainted with all the antiques that had traveled west in covered wagons (even though we knew most of the goods destined for the west would have been jettisoned long before they reached Nebraska), but we respected how precious these items were in their owners' eyes. It was a vital lesson. (Maybe those moments reminded us of our parents' wedding gifts that had been so casually sold.)

My résumé was rapidly expanding when I became a sign painter that year for the new Hudson automobile dealer in Wahoo. He had telephoned the school to inquire if any student was available to create a sign for Hudson Motors, and I readily volunteered. Looking back, I marvel at my readiness to take on any job regardless of my lack of training. I remember, probably because I got as much paint on my clothes as I did on the sign, that it was brown. But I'll never forget that job in particular because I was beginning to develop my lifelong love of anything automotive, and consequently, even such a remote connection to the luxurious Hudson captivated me. It brought me closer to my hopes of one day owning a car. It kept my dreams alive.

When Duane and I weren't in classes or working, we were free to use our time as we wished, and we knew it was easy to hitchhike to Omaha. The first two years we were at Luther, we caught a ride as far as the bus station where we engaged in the sport of people watching during our Thanksgiving and Christmas breaks. There was always a colorful crowd—small children tugging excitedly on the hands of weary parents, elderly men and women dragging heavy suitcases and shopping bags spilling over with brightly wrapped packages, anxious couples gripping each other's hands and perhaps wondering if the future in-laws would approve of them. There was once a family whose path through the milling crowd was marked by the unmistakable juices leaking from their holiday turkey and another who was grappling with a Christmas tree complete with its ball of roots. Duane and I wondered if they had to buy a bus ticket so it could have its own seat, since it clearly wouldn't fit in the luggage compartment under the bus. Children would perch on the wooden benches as their parents handed around sandwiches and apples and their grandparents read the same story over and over again. "Is the bus coming? When are we leaving?" The children would fuss, and fathers would try not to look at their watches in the hopes that another quarter hour had passed since the last plaintive query. Long lines extended from the doorways of the restrooms where mothers juggled diaper bags and babies.

The bus station was an exciting place to be in the 1940s. That was how Americans traveled if they didn't have a car, and if you said "Greyhound," everyone knew you were talking about the bus line and not the dog. Bus transportation was never considered to be glamorous, but it was available, and cheap, and safe. Duane and I loved the excitement, and the noise, and the color; we loved the travelers and the human drama we read in their faces. "I don't know why," I used to say to Duane, "but it makes me happy just to look at them and wonder where they're going." I never thought, "Wait a minute, we don't have a family." And even when we were hungry, we never envied the children who were sucking candy canes or drinking Cokes the parents eventually purchased to quiet their cranky offspring. I was happy for the people that they had some place to go, and neither of us ever begrudged them their happiness. I don't know what drew us to those bustling depots as each holiday approached, but I guess it beat spending Christmas in the basement as we had done all too often.

For some reason, the police never bothered us. We must have looked pretty harmless, and we changed our seats often so they wouldn't notice us. I think they might still have been a little more lenient about permitting travelers to sleep there, because it wasn't that long since the bus stations had been filled with returning veterans.

On another trip to Omaha, as we walked downtown enjoying our usual round of people watching around lunchtime, I remember noting the crowds of men dressed in trim suits with white shirts and colorful ties. I wondered what it would like to be so prosperous that one could wear such attire on a daily basis, and how I would feel if I had a job at the telephone building nearby. Little did I realize then, that those musings were almost prophetic about my future life.

But back in Wahoo, we still worked most weekends on Saturdays. Sundays were still family days and times of quiet recreation in the forties; it would be several years before stores stayed open seven days a week and malls dotted the landscapes and highways. Except for that one lapse when Mrs. Benson caught us in our mild fib about attending vespers, we always attended church. A good friend, Ted Blomquist who frequently enlivened us with his antics, frequently joined us. Ted's parents, who lived in Chicago, had enough money to make other arrangements for his food and lodging on weekends, but he liked to attend worship with us.

One Saturday, Ted, Duane and I decided to stay up all night just to see if we could, but when we went to get him for services the next morning, we found him sound asleep. "I'm coming, I'm coming," he insisted as we none too gently shook him awake before the three of us set off. Since it was a communion Sunday, we joined the line up the middle aisle after the sermon, our eyes piously cast down to avoid distracting each other. As we approached the communion rail, one gentleman was already ahead of us, so Ted, Duane and I followed him, and we all knelt and bowed our heads in prayer. After receiving communion, we stood up and walked back to our pew. As we sat down, we discovered Ted was no longer with us. Duane, who worried more than I did about looking conspicuous, went back to the communion rail, and there was Ted, hanging over the railing with his hands folded as if praying. In fact, he was sound asleep! Duane knelt beside him and carefully nudged him awake. They both stood and returned to our pew. We had a good laugh, and he had a red face. He'd managed to stay up all night—but not all morning.

Ted's dad worked for the Rock Island Railroad as an engineer, and during the Christmas break of 1948 he invited us to his home in Chicago for the vacation. We counted off the days on our calendar as the semester ended, eagerly awaiting this unexpected treat, although we were a little apprehensive about what to expect.

We weren't quite the country bumpkins who had arrived in Wahoo in 1946, but we had never been in a city as large as Chicago, and the pictures we had seen were a little daunting. The streets looked dangerously crowded with cars and buses and trucks, and we worried how we would ever navigate all that traffic. The skyscrapers appeared awesomely high to us, much taller than any grain elevator we had ever seen, and the sidewalks were wider than many country roads. Even getting a ride in a friend's Jeep to Omaha and catching the train there added to our excitement, since in the past we had traveled on feeder lines and spurs with old equipment, not the streamlined passenger cars we'd be riding now.

Any qualms we had about our visit proved to be groundless, as Ted's mother was the most hospitable woman we had yet met. Ted must have told her a little about our early life because as soon as she met us at the station, she made us feel as if she'd known us for a long time and was glad we had come. She seemed to understand that we would enjoy a quick hug or pat on the shoulder but wouldn't know what to do if she tried to kiss us goodnight.

Mrs. Blomquist made marvelous chocolate pudding and mashed potatoes with lots of butter and no lumps, and she didn't complain how often she had to wash our clothes so that we always had clean shirts and pants for the week of our visit. She even re-patched the places where Duane and I had tried to mend the worn-out elbows. Best of all, she had bought us a few practical gifts to put under their tree; they were so gaily wrapped, we didn't realize they were more necessities than luxuries.

Although Ted's father had to work most of the time we were in Chicago, he invited us to see the rail yards, and we had a lot to tell the boys back at school about the locomotives he allowed us to board. Getting the engineer's view of the tracks was an entirely different perspective from standing on the platform.

Some days we just enjoyed lying in bed in the mornings, and when we learned that Ted had his own wake-up-to-music radio, we were content to pull up the covers and enjoy the programs. We never felt jealous that Ted, who was adopted, enjoyed privileges we had never had. We just considered it a rare treat to spend a few hours after breakfast playing cards or staying indoors out of the cold Chicago winds, instead of having to go look for a job. We had thought the time spent at Edna Nelson's had been a vacation, but now we were learning the real meaning of the word *relaxation*.

Mrs. Blomquist had given us a list of places she thought we should visit, and we must have gone to at least one museum, but most of the trip remains a pleasant haze, with one great exception. As part of the holiday celebrations and as a special Christmas gift, Ted's mother had arranged for us to attend Don Ameche's *Welcome Travelers* radio program, a quiz show that was specifically geared to out-of-towners.

Imagine our surprise when we were selected from the audience to become contestants. It was fortunate we hadn't known ahead of time that we would be chosen, so we had no time to grow jittery at the prospect. The program aired on WBBM from the famed College Inn restaurant at the Hotel Sherman, where we sat in amazement ogling the extravagant décor. We almost missed the show we were so enthralled with the magnificent marble lobby.

The climax of the day occurred when we each won a pair of stadium boots—now we had two pairs of shoes, a rare novelty in our lives. For the first time, we had real protection from the snow and sleet. Our hearts and our feet would treasure that Christmas week in Chicago for a long, long time.

Chapter Nineteen
Family Failings

The visit to Ted's family, letters from our sisters, and watching the holiday travelers must have awakened a dormant need to reconnect with more family. Perhaps we hungered to replace the attachments, tenuous as they had been, that we had lost when Dad had abandoned us in Wahoo in 1946. Fresh from the loving relationships we had admired at Ted's, the echoing hallways of the dormitories seemed particularly desolate to our vulnerable morale, and we yearned for warmth and affection.

Whatever the impetus, one day we walked about a mile from the bus station in Omaha in search of the house where we had learned from Ruth that our mother's sister, Aunt Anna Hassel, lived. It was a disastrous decision for hungry spirits. I can see us now, two unkempt youngsters with shaggy hair and pants above their ankles, stepping up to the front door and jabbing the doorbell. What did we anticipate on the other side of that door? Our appearance was enough to frighten any elderly woman. Did we believe this almost unknown aunt would throw open her door with a cry of delight or even a hint of recognition? Aunt Anna Hassel had never tried to contact us; she might not even know we had come to Omaha. There was nothing in our past, only dogged optimism for the future, to encourage us to expect open arms of welcome from any of our relatives. Fortunately, we had armored our defenses against disappointment so often we were subconsciously ready for disappointment, although we weren't past the point of hurt.

I can see her now, pulling the drape aside, peering through the glass and then letting the curtain drop back into place. She had stared at us with a questioning glance that was followed by a look of suspicion as if to say "They've found me." We could almost hear the sound of the drapery falling over the window to block her face and the echo of her footsteps on her bare floors as she moved away from us. Maybe she thought we were two tramps looking for a handout. I don't think so. The hard truth was that long ago, after our father died, the family had decided that we were two orphans they were better off ignoring. Now that we were older, I imagine they thought that if they were kind to us, we might latch on to them and become another burden for them to carry. If Aunt Anna had any question about our identity, she wouldn't take any chances it was us—just in case.

We trudged away from her house defeated in our attempt to reconnect with another family member, but the sight of her sour face didn't quite dampen our enthusiasm or prevent us from seeking out other relatives. During those years at Luther we were occasionally invited to visit our Uncle Carl, and we usually went even though these were often unpleasant afternoons. I'm not sure if the invitations were issued out of a sense of obligation or if he saw these moments as a chance to inflate his ego and impress us with his possessions.

Not quite a ne'er do well, Carl drifted from job to job, never quite a failure but never developing a professional career. He spent any extra income he had, especially when he received his discount as a salesman at KK Appliances, on the latest gadgets or toys for Phillip. "Phillip," he would whine, when we visited, "show Ed and Duane the phonograph we gave you for Christmas," or "maybe the boys would like to see your new bicycle," or "go get the sports jacket your mother just bought." But he never suggested that maybe we'd like to listen, or ride, or borrow.

It was Uncle Carl who had suggested that we be sent to an orphanage after our father died, and I think he might have harbored a grudge that he had lost that battle when Dad took us back to Canada. He must have hoped that someone else would adopt us, and that we could be cut off completely from his family tree. His antipathy toward us deepened with the reading of his mother's will, and his disappointment festered. At her death, she had bequeathed her family's farm to my sisters and us, and to Uncle Carl's great chagrin, Phillip had received nothing. Our grandmother might have felt that as orphans we needed greater financial protection than our cousin, although she didn't take into consideration that Carl was a poor provider for his family.

From then on, he never lost an opportunity to belittle us or to ensure that we didn't profit from any good fortune in which Phillip had no share. Uncle Carl had recognized a perfect opportunity when, as the executor of our grandmother's estate, he neglected to pay the required property taxes on her farm. Within a few years the state foreclosed on it, and we thereby lost both the potential income and the pride of ownership. He had even managed to dip into the postal savings account of approximately $2,000 that had been left in trust for us and to confiscate it for his own use. "Do you think," I once inquired of one of my sisters, "that Uncle Carl was afraid we'd find out about his dishonesty if we visited too often and became too friendly with Phillip or Aunt Elizabeth?"

Aunt Elizabeth was actually Uncle Carl's first cousin, a relationship that should certainly have barred their marriage, and she was a kindly, if ineffectual, woman. One year while we were in Wahoo, she sent us a homemade cake for our birthday—we had finally found out when that was – and I remember she packed it in popcorn. She'd obviously noticed that our pants were too short and our cuffs fraying at the edges because she included some old clothes of Phillip's. When we mistakenly thanked her in his hearing, Uncle Carl was furious. Aunt Elizabeth sat there cowering in the face of his scathing criticism and barrage of scorn. He was a man who angered easily, particularly if he thought "those nephews of mine" had benefitted from his immediate family. He was no relation of Aunt Hildore, but his personality bore a strong resemblance.

Duane and I suspected that Phillip's character was basically weak and that he tended to lean in the direction of the strongest wind. We were sure we were right when he told us, "I really loved Alice," but he couldn't explain why he had never stood up for her when she had moved in with them after Grandmother Carlson died. He was much like his mother. I don't think he ever had dreams like mine, or else he lacked the will to pursue them. He was, however, a talented musician who attended Hastings College and succeeded so well that he earned a scholarship to study music in Austria. There, he fell in love with a girl whom he convinced to come to the United States, where they would marry. Unfortunately, neither of them had reckoned on the other arrangements that his father had made for his future.

Following his mercenary inclinations, Carl had handpicked another young woman, who everyone expected would inherit several sections of farmland that he coveted, to be Phillip's bride. Without much argument, the young man had acceded to his father and abandoned his Austrian sweetheart in favor of this young lady. As it turned out, no one benefited from Uncle Carl's interference, for shortly after the marriage and the young couple's move to Colorado, the bride died prematurely of cancer. Her aging relatives left their property to other heirs.

Poor Phillip couldn't win. A newspaper obituary reported the coming burial service in Holdrege, and while Phillip was attending the funeral in Nebraska, his house in Denver was completely ransacked. The neighbors, who questioned the drivers of the trailer backed up to Phillip's house, believed their response, "Oh, he's moving back to Nebraska."

Phillip's life didn't improve immeasurably after that, for like his father he never prospered in business. I was always saddened that he had listened to Uncle Carl rather than pursue his talent for music, a direction that might have made him a happier man, if not necessarily a wealthier one.

Chapter Twenty
Money Matters

The four years at Luther Academy broadened our view of the world in many ways, although at times I regret now that we ignored some of the opportunities. Even though neither of us pursued our studies diligently, we admired classmates like Phil Youngquist who actually seemed to enjoy challenging math puzzles or the beauty of a well-turned phrase.

I found a much needed hero in the person of S. O. Johnson, one of the few teachers who stand out in my mind. I'm sure he recognized that we felt as if we didn't quite fit in, and he offered us the warmth of his heart as well as practical knowledge. He never passed us in the hallways or walking across the paths to Old Main without a greeting or a quick salute. He filled the role of affectionate fatherly critic we needed and gave us a model to emulate.

I'm quite certain that S. O., as he was known to everyone at Luther, recognized that his mechanical engineering classes had aroused the only academic passion I felt, and that they might have spurred me on to continued study if more advanced courses had been available. With his eclectic approach to life that made learning almost fun, S. O. knew instinctively that boys who found syntax and grammar boring would immediately perk up in Swedish class if he mixed in feats of early Scandinavian warriors or figures from folklore.

If I'd known the term at the time, I would have called him a Renaissance man, since he had so many interests and skills. He is probably best remembered by scores of alumni for the simple but beautiful stone arch he designed and constructed for the entrance to Luther College. However, I remember him best for the generous loan (which I reveal later in this chapter) he offered to me shortly before I left school.

Although Luther opened up new horizons, Duane and I were so busy honing simple survival techniques that we didn't have much energy left for leisure activities. In truth, we lacked the two most important resources—time and money—to cultivate the friendship of girls or purchase tickets for football games or dances. In addition, we had neither the kinds of clothes nor the flashy cars that attracted coeds.

"I don't think she'd want to go out with me, do you, Duane?" I'd ask about a particular girl. Never too sure whether it was better to agree or to disagree—and probably because we'd have to pool our clothes to achieve one outfit decent enough for any girl to be seen with us—he'd usually concur. So instead of socializing with classmates who lived near Wahoo, when the weekend came we'd mosey down to the gas station in search of work or to hang out with the locals. There was almost always someone else with more time than money like us, and we still got greater satisfaction from earning money than earning grades. We had also developed passing friendships with some of our employers and often shared more common interests with them than we did with our fellow students. Put another way, we often identified more closely with town than gown.

By the time graduation loomed in June 1950, we didn't have any firm plans for the future beyond spending the next two years enrolled in Luther's college program. Our teachers had basically given up on us, and S. O. had developed health setbacks that prevented us from approaching him for guidance. About the only careers familiar to us were farming and the ministry. Life at the Carlsons' and my summers of farming in Beaver City had taught me the fragility of a life dependent on agriculture, and although I loved my church, I didn't want to scrape by as Dad had, driving from hamlet to hamlet each weekend to preach. I also recognized that to support the inner drive that had prompted me to buy those meals for the down-and-outs in Beaver City would require a profession that promised material success. I had had enough of doing without, but I wasn't yet set on the path that would lead me to prosperity.

To this day, I can't understand why I was never jealous of people who clearly had more money than I did, but I was beginning to think that one day I would like to be one of those people who could hop on a bus and travel to new places. I just didn't know how to achieve those goals, and with S. O. ill, there was no one who seemed poised to point me in the right direction.

Wealth, Duane and I were learning, is an important element in getting ahead. We didn't crave power, but we knew that with a good job and a steady paycheck we would gain respect. Enough cash to buy a doll might equal riches to a youngster whose home is in a cellar, and fifty cents might satisfy the same boy shopping for a memento on a trip to his new country, but at this stage of life, we were gaining new insight into the value of money. We were soon going to learn the difficult lesson that money can only be spent once.

At the end of each semester, our grades were sent to Dad in Canada, and he probably received an accounting of our scholarship funds as well as the disposition of the $3,700 which we had inherited from the sale of our parents' assets. However, we had little concept of the expenses involved in our education or the difference in the costs of room, and board, and books. Day-to-day living we could handle, but like most teenagers, we didn't have a grasp of the big picture and never gave a thought to our dwindling funds. Shortly before the end of our senior year, however, the school treasurer, V. E. Johnson, sent for us, and that day we had our first serious lesson in accounting. It may have been the most memorable instruction we had at Luther, or at least the one that had the greatest impact.

"Ed and Duane," he started out, as if to let us down easily, "it's been such a pleasure to have the sons of Pastor Vikman attending Luther Academy. I'm sure if he was still alive, he'd be proud of how independent and self-reliant you have become. I feel confident your years here have prepared you well for a successful life, no matter what course you choose."

We probably squirmed a little in our chairs because we knew our class standing was in the bottom quarter, and Mr. Johnson was stretching the truth if he was praising our academic record. We might not have been astute about finances, but we knew enough about people by then to recognize when someone was sugarcoating a situation. With a wry glance at one another, we waited to hear the bad news. Mr. Johnson continued, "I guess there is no way to break this to you gently, but there is almost no money left in the scholarship fund for your tuition."

We learned that we would graduate from the high school at Luther as expected, but now we were almost broke. The riches we had inherited, the money we thought had made us millionaires, had dwindled to just a couple of hundred dollars. Money well spent, to be sure, but nevertheless, there was little left to jingle in our pockets beyond the small sums we could earn.

What lay ahead was one big question mark. We might have been country bumpkins in a lot of ways, but living on our own for the past four years had broadened our vision. We knew it would take a lot more than the sale of crow claws and gopher tails to put dinner on the table in the days and years ahead, and it was time to put our imaginations and brains to work. Two dejected boys wandered back to the dormitory, oblivious to the joyous voices of classmates celebrating their last examinations and the prospect of summer fun to come.

We had assumed we would complete the college curriculum that Luther offered, even though we had barely succeeded with the high school courses. Now V. E. Johnson had told us that both our savings and our scholarship funds were nearly depleted. There might be enough for one of us to continue, but that was all.

We hardly noticed the other boys lugging their suitcases back to their rooms to pack with all the clothes and gear accumulated since September. Every so often, one of them would punch us on an arm, jovially exclaiming, "Great to be getting out, hey, Vikman?" Or, "Got any plans? Got a good job lined up?" It was easy to tell who knew us best by their questions. Only casual acquaintances thought we would be able to travel or relax before fall came. They ate when meals were served and had no idea that some people worked, made a buck, and then ate. Soon the last classes and exams were over, and the rest of the seniors piled into their cars with their exultant parents.

The day after commencement, Duane and I sat in our room in the empty dormitory and contemplated our future. "What are we going to do now?" I asked Duane. "I thought we had all the money we needed to last for two more years."

For a long time that night we hunched on our bunk beds, picking each other's brains for a way out of our predicament, but as the hours passed, we hadn't found a solution. We knew we wanted to take care of each other, so we tossed around the idea of Duane—he found studying even more arduous than I did—getting a job while I stayed in school, and we faced the realization that we might have to live in different places. We had only considered the idea of eventual separation in a theoretical way, but now it became a distinct possibility. It was scary to ponder and finally, finding that no clear cut answer came to mind, we decided to call it a night. Maybe a little sleep would help.

When we didn't have any better idea by the next morning, we wandered into town in search of breakfast, and there, on a newsstand, we found the solution to our problem. "President Truman announced today that he has ordered United States air and naval forces to fight with South Korea's Army," read the headline. Duane's eyes lit up at the announcement, and I knew at

148

once what he was going to do. Long lines hadn't yet formed at the recruiting station when Duane presented himself, and it didn't take a recruiter long to administer the oath for enlisted men. Hardly any time had passed at all before I stood watching as my beloved identical twin raised his right arm and recited: "I, Duane Gustav Vikman, do solemnly swear that I will support the constitution of the United States." My eyes brimmed with tears as he continued, "do solemnly swear to bear true allegiance to the United States of America, and to serve them honestly and faithfully, against all their enemies or opposers whatsoever, and to observe and obey the orders of the President of the United States of America, and the orders of the officers appointed over me." With that affirmation, Duane had also confirmed the decision that would result in the longest separation of our lives and would put unknown miles and an ocean between us. The rest of the summer after Duane left Wahoo is mostly a hazy memory of the usual odd jobs that filled my days. I returned to school in the fall with little enthusiasm.

I soon realized I still didn't find any subjects that excited me during my first year in the college program. I wandered aimlessly through a labyrinth of courses I didn't understand, unsure why I had elected to stay. Then one day I received a message to make an appointment with the treasurer. Facing him alone in his office, his desk neatly piled high with his ledgers, I discovered to my dismay that not only had all the money been spent, but that I WAS IN DEBT! "But, but," I stammered, interrupting what was obviously a painful speech for him. "I thought there was enough money…" "Edwin," he broke in before I could finish my sentence, "prices have increased alarmingly since the war ended in '45." His usually cheerful face warned me with its dour look, his smile fading as he continued, "I'm afraid the accounting I gave you of your available funds was a bit optimistic. In reviewing your status, I originally found the monies available for your tuition were dangerously low. Actually, before you came in I was going over the totals one more time, and I regret to tell you that you actually owe Luther College $200."

Two hundred dollars! I was stunned. How could this have happened? Duane and I thought we had resolved the problems of our immediate future when he had enlisted, and we had trusted these administrators implicitly. They were learned and knowledgeable men, skilled (or so we assumed) in the management of the financial affairs of the college.

We had proven ourselves to be practical stewards of the small sums we had earned throughout the years, but we were novices when it came to handling larger amounts. We had relied on the superior experience of these men, and now I was hearing V. E. Johnson had made a mistake.

I didn't know what to say or think. I was totally confused at this turn of events. I thought of a scene I had once admired in a book that showed logs careening dangerously down a rushing stream towards the falls with absolutely no way of stopping before the final drop. I felt as if I was one of the logs, and I could only mutter, "I'm broke! Not only that, I'm in debt. Forgive us our debts as we forgive our debtors."

I had prayed that often, and now in a practical sense I hoped someone would hear and come to my aid. To my utter amazement, but unbounded gratitude, my savior came in the form of my old mentor, S. O. Johnson. Duane and I had always thought of him as a friend and once, knowing his fondness for chicken wings, I had taken some to him when he was in the hospital. I had been proud to show my affection for him when I bought them from my small store of savings. Now, he was showing his affection at a critical juncture for me when, hearing of my plight, he brought me the $200 needed to restore my solvency.

It was like an angel had heard my prayers—S. O. was by then a pretty old man, but he was also astute, and I think he was one of the first individuals who understood that I would outgrow my past and amount to something. I had never told him of my dream—it was still a little too vague to share—but he was helping me to keep it alive. But before it could happen, however, I had some key decisions to reach.

Jotted down on paper, the facts didn't look promising to me. I was bored, I was broke, and I was bereft of the only caring family member I knew. During our few earlier separations, Duane and I had always known that we would be reunited in just a few short weeks or months, but since Duane had enlisted, we hadn't been able to plan a similar reunion. We knew his leaves and my vacations would probably rarely coincide, and we had parted with little expectations.

Now I returned to my room—for some reason I had never been assigned a roommate—and stared at the empty mattress. The stripes on the ticking blurred through the tears I couldn't quite wipe away as I contemplated this new situation. Even worse, I had never had to make this kind of choice on my own. In the midst of a dormitory teeming with young men boisterously recounting their latest feats on the gridiron or bemoaning the *C* they had earned on a recent paper, I felt isolated and strangely alone. The pounding of feet in the corridor outside my door and the cheerful noise barely penetrated my solitude.

I missed my twin as only another twin can, given the extraordinary bond that exists from the womb. I finally reached the only conclusion that seemed obvious and logical to me: I would join the navy and maybe someday Duane and I could be back together. At the same time, I promised myself that I would work hard and save my money, and one day I would pay back the $200 to S. O. And I did. At about that time—and maybe it was due to S. O's faith in me—I started to recapture my dream.

Chapter Twenty One
Naval Maneuvers

Funny, isn't it, that two farm boys who had never even learned to swim, joined the navy? Even stranger still, I found out later, landlocked Wahoo, Nebraska, had a submarine named after it. Life does have its quirks!

I followed Duane to boot camp in San Diego, although he, of course, had moved on to more exotic ports long before I arrived. Each of us, again not knowing what the future might hold, had returned to Edmonton following boot camp to spend our last two weeks with Dad before shipping out. It seems an odd choice today, for we had certainly suffered whenever we lived under his roof, but we could never forget he was our father's brother, and his house was the only place we might call home.

Our visits to Edmonton marked the first occasion each of us had to see Dad and Aunt Hildore after he had driven us to Axtell in 1946. Now that I have a lifetime of experience behind me, I have more questions than answers about the years Duane and I lived with them. The barren basement, standing up at mealtimes, being farmed out to any family looking for cheap labor— why had this constant cruelty marred our childhood? Since Dad and Aunt Hildore were the only family we had known consistently, I don't question our going back to see them, but I do wonder at the welcome that occurred when we returned. And now that I have been happily married for many years, I have questions about their relationship to one another that I never entertained as a boy. It didn't occur to me then that I never saw them exchange hugs or other signs of endearment—although I did see them occasionally kiss Miriam or Linnea. I recognize now the tension that existed between them and that Dad, in particular, seemed wary of how he spoke or reacted. It was if he was concerned about provoking her anger or causing a scene.

I had noticed one subtle change in Dad's more recent letters when Mom, as he had always referred to her, had started adding postscripts, using that title as her signature. We really hadn't called her anything since our attempt, as toddlers, to call her mother when she had rebuffed us so sharply. In fact, we had rarely addressed her directly at all, but now we gave in and called her Mom. It was easier for everyone. Sometime in the past year, she had even started writing her own letters to us saying, "We would like you to come home." But even so, I was flabbergasted and bewildered at her new attitude.

Mom and Dad had moved to a different house, which happily spared me from revisiting the ugly scenes of my childhood. I wasn't surprised to find that my room in the new home was still in the basement, but luxury of luxuries, I discovered I had a bathroom down there all to myself while I visited!

My furlough was a whirlwind of activities, with a welcome home party hosted by Hildur and Astrid Carlson from the church, going out to dinners with other parishioners, and catching up with other young men and women I remembered from Cromdale School. I wore my naval uniform and thoroughly enjoyed the adulation of being an American sailor in Canada. It felt good to be the center of attention where I had once felt invisible.

Duane had told me what to expect in the way of festivities, but even so I was overwhelmed by the greetings from people who had previously barely noticed me, except as the pastor's nephew. My aunt apparently had told everyone she knew that I would be visiting, and their response had been to host one celebration after another. My aunt's effusive conversation must have seemed strange to some people after the years she had ignored us, but I was just grateful for the outpouring of love and affection and thought, "The awful stuff is over."

Later, I wondered if Mom might be regretting some of her earlier behavior and was actually feathering her nest just in case she became dependent on us as she aged. In Hildore, the word *hypocrite* plumbed new meanings. She was aware that Miriam's husband was a missionary who couldn't be counted on for support, and Linnea would always be too busy to notice any needs but her own.

However, my Canadian idyll soon ended, and before long I was on a ship and heading for the Inchon invasion. Even after enduring the hardships of my youth, I wasn't prepared for the horrors of battle; I don't suppose anyone ever is, and I badly wanted to get another assignment. To my great surprise, I was sent back to the United States on a different tour of duty. I thought, "How lucky can I be?"

I soon found myself in Bremerton, Washington, but my good fortune was of short duration, as I was then assigned to an LST, a type of naval vessel created during World War II to support amphibious operations. The vessel was loaded with 350 tons of land mines and explosives, which was not the most comfortable of cargoes, as we soon found out. Somewhere in the western Pacific, we tried valiantly to ride out a typhoon, but the heaving seas and mountainous waves proved too much for our ship. The load shifted, and we came perilously close to being permanent citizens of Davy Jones's locker. When the storm passed, and the captain had assessed the damage, we headed to Pearl Harbor and Hickam Air Force Base. Fifty men got liberty, and I was lucky to be one of them.

As it turned out, I was about to become much luckier than I could ever have hoped. Duane has recorded some of his experiences in the navy, and the following account based on his diary describes a remarkable anecdote of how our lives again merged. We had been apart for two years at that point, and his absence from my life had been painful.

After Duane left boot camp in San Diego, he first reported to Treasure Island in San Francisco before traveling to Pearl Harbor on the Daniel I. Sultan, a transport ship named after the former inspector general of the army. (These ships had been decommissioned by the navy after World War II and transferred to the army where they were renamed after the army's own personnel. When in 1950 they reverted to the navy, they retained their army name.)

In Hawaii, Duane waited for further orders directing him to serve on one of the many ships engaged in the Korean conflict. During the interim, a chance acquaintanceship with a first-class petty officer aboard the Sultan led to significant changes in our lives.

Fortunately for us, this officer, Ralph Burba, became secretary to the captain of Air Transport Squadron Eight, an officer whose connections would prove invaluable to Duane and me. For reasons still unknown to Duane, Burba had mentioned his name to Captain Clifton and perhaps related some of our background as well.

As Duane recounts the story, he was alone in his room (only in Hawaii did sailors have accommodations for two), about four in the afternoon one Sunday when another sailor knocked and entered. At first he didn't recognize the man, but then he realized that it was me. I was on my second trip to the Korean peninsula, and had stopped by in hopes of seeing him.

After embracing each other excitedly and a quick conversation to catch each other up on our recent activities, Duane's next thought was to take me over to the captain's office to introduce me to him. Even today, he doesn't know what hopes prompted this move. Our visit was short, however, because I had to get back to my ship that was due to leave later that day.

Soon after we parted, the officer of the day told Duane that Captain Clifton wanted to see him immediately in his office. Duane was scared to death, for he was worried he might have overstepped his bounds and seemed too familiar with his superior. What occurred next was almost slapstick comedy in the speed with which it happened, as the captain remarked, "I'm surprised you and your brother aren't stationed together." Duane replied, "I would really like that, but Ed has asked for a transfer three times and has always been turned down."

The captain continued, "Would you like your brother here with you?" When Duane responded affirmatively, Captain Clifton next asked, "Can you type?" Duane admitted he could, but not very well. Then the captain added, "Take this dictation quickly, and as soon as it's ready, I'll sign it." It took Duane nine attempts to type the letter without errors for Captain Clifton's signature. There was no whiteout or computerized backspacing in those days to simplify this task.

When the document was signed, Captain Clifton continued, "Since you don't have much time, take my jeep and get to Military Air Transport Squadron immediately. Admiral Hoskins will be waiting for you and will have his endorsement ready." Duane sped to where Admiral Hoskins was waiting for him, but he wasn't yet finished with navy protocol, and was told, "Now you have to take this to Admiral Radford at CincPac [Commander in Chief of the Pacific Feet] for his final approval. Don't dare be late, because he waits for no one." When Duane arrived there, Admiral Radford personally handed him the endorsement and said, "I hope this will help your cause." Duane thanked him, and left for my ship. Our time was almost up, but, of course, I knew nothing of what was transpiring.

When Duane arrived at the LST, he was met by the chief petty officer, and more questions and comedy ensued. First he explained to the officer that he had orders to transfer one of his men, but he was met with an amused glance as if to say "you're crazy." Frustrated that he had to go through the proper chain of command when he knew he had so little time, Duane was then taken to the acting captain (actually a lieutenant) who hollered, "Nobody is going to leave this ship!"

As he began reading the document, the captain was unmoved, but the expression on his face changed when he saw the endorsement from Admiral Hoskins. When he saw the signature from the highest naval officer, namely Admiral Radford [CinPac], it was, as the saying goes, all over but the shouting. And shouting there was.

The captain sent for me, reaming me out for what he thought I had planned while I was on temporary leave from his command and screaming, "Get off my ship!"

Totally amazed at this turn of events, I rushed to my bunk and packed my personal belongings, and we left for Air Transport Squadron Eight. But the comedy still had one more act, one more military snafu. When I went to check in, I was told by the officer of the day, "I cannot accept you here because the orders read, Military Air Transport Squadron." We were crestfallen, since these orders meant I had to get to the other side of Oahu, and there was no time for that. Sadly, Duane then took me back to my LST, but he wasn't defeated yet.

He immediately went back to Hickam Air Force Base and got the orders changed to read Hickam Air Force Base Air Transport Squadron Eight. Scrambling back into the captain's jeep, he again headed back to the LST. By now, he had only five minutes to present the new orders because my ship was due to weigh anchor, and SHIPS LEAVE ON TIME.

Later, Duane told me that the next few minutes seemed like hours as he waited for me. The railings were put up, the houser lines taken down, and a small tractor hooked up to the gangway. Still I didn't appear. He was worried for me because he realized what I would face if I sailed on the ship. This was wartime, and I could have been court-martialed if anyone thought I was attempting to countermand my original orders.

Just then fate intervened. The gangway had shifted about five feet, so the driver got off to make sure everything was okay. I appeared and was up and over the railings as the gangway was starting to move. As I landed on the moving passageway, the driver mercifully stopped. I walked down the steps and got into the Jeep. Duane gunned the motor, and we left for Hickam Air Force Base, where I was accepted for my new assignment. The comedy was over. A thought came to me, "This isn't a dream. I think I'm beginning to make it."

Just two weeks later, I learned that my ship had been blown up off the Korean peninsula, and there were no survivors.

Duane's relationship with Captain Clifton continued to smooth the seas for us, as he encouraged both of us to take advantage of the advancement possibilities offered by the navy. We both enrolled at the U.S. Armed Forces Institute for several months to prepare for the examinations for promotion. The difficulties we had both experienced since our first day at school meant long hours of study at night and constant use of the dictionary to augment our deficient vocabulary. We faced the day of our exam with great trepidation and sweaty hands, and, unfortunately, Duane didn't pass, while I did. He remained a seaman, and I advanced to the rank of petty officer third class. The extra semester I had studied at Luther College, when Duane had enlisted, had possibly given me an extra edge.

Some people who grow up in total penury as Duane and I did become committed skin flints the minute they earn any money, but I prefer to think that we just possessed a frugal streak. During our stint in Honolulu, the two of us would walk to Waikiki Beach to save the twenty-five cent bus fare; we never bought even a coke at the USO and rarely spent money on girls. We always had cash in our pockets, and our friends referred to us as the gold dust twins or their own Honolulu Savings and Loan.

At that point, we had been working all our adult lives—actually most of our childhood years as well—and the only rewards we had ever received had come from our own endeavors. We knew better than to squander our hard-earned dollars in one Saturday night fling or in a series of ill-considered and fleeting extravagances. We'd seen too many of our fellow sailors more than a little the worse for wear after they'd wasted a week's pay on a Saturday night of bar hopping, or a few hours at the poker table, or, sadder still, a combination of the two. We'd also loaned our shoulders to morning-after tears when other guys looked disbelievingly at their empty wallets, grateful if they found a spare two bits to get their shirts from the laundry.

I had my dream, and I knew that building a nest egg would help bring its fulfillment. Intent as we were on saving our pay, we had little excitement to liven up our days, but one episode in particular brightened up our patch of the Pacific.

In January 1954, Marilyn Monroe and Joe DiMaggio flew to Japan on their honeymoon and stopped in Hawaii while the crew refueled their airplane. One of my buddies, a photographer, heard through the grapevine that the famous lovebirds were in a secluded area at the airport during their layover. He proposed driving over there to try to get some pictures of Marilyn, and he invited me to join him. Of course, I jumped at the chance. There wasn't a guy on Oahu who wouldn't have seized the opportunity to be in the same airspace as that sex goddess, so I leaped into his Jeep for the ride.

Hawaii was still a territory then, and tourism hadn't yet become a staple industry there, so the airport wasn't a busy place. We soon found the special room where Marilyn's agent permitted pictures to be taken. When my buddy had finished with the shoot, he was allowed to take all his film with him, with the proviso that he develop only one print and then destroy the negatives. He kept his promise, but when he had finished in the darkroom, he held up some of the shots, saying, "Hey, Ed, I can't use these. Do you want them?" (They included some of her bandaged and splinted thumb, which she later told questioning fans she had "bumped," although many people thought DiMggio was the culprit.) I grinned from ear to ear, and I packed those four black and white photos safely among the most treasured mementoes in my navy album.

Chapter Twenty Two
Another Goodbye

Nothing, neither the beauty of the swaying palm trees silhouetted against a cerulean sky, nor the gentle thrum of the ukuleles which pervaded the streets of Waikiki, could mask the ever-present thoughts of the war being waged on the far side of the ocean. How could it, with the massive ships weighing anchor and disappearing over the horizon to who knew what fate, and planes taking off each day toward the west? The beachside streets teemed with throngs of battered servicemen enjoying the short days of R&R before returning to battle. Our buddies had brothers and fathers and even sisters serving, and I knew they dreaded the summons to their superiors' offices that meant awful news had come. Duane and I had no such fears with no siblings to worry about, so we were totally unnerved when we learned that a telegram dated April 14, 1953, had arrived for us.

It read, simply, *"DAD IN HOSPITAL SERIOUSLY ILL FROM HEART ATTACK HAVE SPECIAL NURSES DOING EVERYTHING POSSIBLE DO AS YOU THINK BEST IF ONE OR BOTH OF YOU CAN GET LEAVE TO COME HOME MOM."*

I was stunned. I had visited them once after the boot camp trip. The two weeks I had spent with them had been hectic, and I guess I had never really looked at Dad carefully. Had he appeared unwell? Had he seemed more tired than usual? Had he felt sick and hadn't wanted to worry me when I was facing an uncertain future? Had my anxiety about shipping off to war without the support of Duane who had been the mainstay of most of my life made me less observant of him? Whatever the answer, there in black and white was disturbing news, and Duane and I scrambled to put in our request for compassionate leave.

We knew Dad had suffered crucial changes that had caused great stress in his life since we had last seen him. During his career, he had worked untiringly to develop the church in Edmonton and had devoted countless hours and days to the Lutheran Church in Canada. He had served as president of the Lutheran Canada Conference and been a member of it for many years. In short, he had earned the respect of congregations and leaders of many churches, and he was justifiably proud of what he had attained.

It is difficult to imagine the depth of his anguish when he learned that the members of his own church—colleagues he had trusted—had begun to question his integrity. Matters came to a head when the board at Augustana Lutheran Church held a secret meeting and asked for his resignation. Measuring his despondency would have been impossible. He had shepherded the church from its infancy at the YWCA to the space at the home of one of the congregants, and his vision of a permanent church in the heart of Edmonton had almost reached fruition. He could not have expected this bombshell.

Since the meeting was held covertly, I will never know exactly what was said that day, but from later conversations with people like Miriam's friend Shirley, I have been able to surmise what transpired. Throughout the years after Duane and I had gone to live with him, neighbors and congregants had noticed our periodic absences but hadn't really questioned them. We had averted any suspicions as well when we insisted that we preferred living in the country to the city, if someone mentioned they had missed us.

Shirley had played at the house often, and I think she might have persuaded Miriam to show her where we slept. She had commented at one of the parties before I shipped out, "I just can't believe how you guys lived! I can never get over how mean 'she' was to you." Shirley never said "your aunt." She might have spread seeds of doubt about our uncle if she broadcast her impressions to others.

I imagine some people may have compared the pretty dresses the girls wore to our worn-out pants and shirts, but if they voiced their concerns, they must have been satisfied with the answers they received. I suspect, too, that most of them had preferred complacent inaction to the trouble they might have caused by indulging their curiosity. Too many questions addressed to their pastor might appear disrespectful.

Perhaps our reappearance after four years in Nebraska, when we visited on our way to the navy, had reminded people of our existence, or perhaps the pomp with which we were shown off awakened suspicions. Whatever the reason, Dad had lost his church, and he and Mom had moved west to Vancouver. The loss of respect and admiration was a blow from which he never completely recovered, and the stress from it probably contributed to his fatal heart attack.

But he possessed a remarkably indomitable spirit, and although almost sixty-seven, he somehow mustered the strength to found yet another church in Burnaby, British Columbia. This time, the congregation met in an old mortuary Dad had purchased, but he and his parishioners succeeded in raising sufficient funds to build a church before he died.

Captain Clifton arranged for us to fly on a seaplane from Honolulu to Seattle, and from there we hitchhiked in uniform. We weren't in time for a last goodbye, but we did arrive in Seattle on the morning he passed away.

The day of Dad's funeral might have been the most surreal of our lives. If we found Mom's behavior in Edmonton difficult to believe, her actions that morning were positively unfathomable. We were exhausted after our trip across the Pacific, and we were both emotionally drained. Duane and I were certainly not prepared for her to appear in the room where we were getting ready for the funeral and ask, as she sat on the edge of the bed, "Boys, can you ever forgive me for the way I treated you?" In our grief and turmoil, we immediately responded, "You're forgiven," although her unexpected contrition had come too late to our lives to foster any true affection for her. In hindsight, I'm amazed we answered as we did, considering that the treatment we received from her when we were children would require immediate social service intervention today. Later, we would speculate if she was already feathering her nest for the future, since such an abrupt change in her behavior seemed otherwise unwarranted. But we didn't have much time to ponder the question more deeply before our leave ended, and when it was over, we returned to Hawaii until we completed our tour of duty.

Chapter Twenty Three
I Can Make It

The "police action," as the Korean War came to be called, dragged on, with the many casualties on the United Nations side vastly overshadowed by the losses of the North Korean and Chinese armies. Finally, the two opposing forces declared an armistice on July 27, 1954. Duane was the first to be mustered out, but my tour of duty ended a few months later. We enjoyed our first taste of deserved indulgence when I joined him in Omaha after my discharge, and we pooled our accumulated savings, planning to buy our own car.

I had long yearned to own my own wheels, and although I had developed great affection for the horses Jerry and Fly at the Carlson farm, I also appreciated the advantages of horsepower over horse power. We had both admired Mr. Dowie's car when we waxed it while at Luther Academy, and the thrill of maneuvering those big rigs and semis at our jobs had been unforgettable. Now that I was close to becoming the owner of my own automobile, I was also learning an important lesson. I had become quite adept at doing without a lot of extras, but now I recognized that the true value of a piggy bank was knowing when to crack it open and savor the contents. Now that the time had come to invest in an automobile, the time had also come to buy only the very best. I have never veered from the belief that quality should always exceed quantity.

Duane and I poured over magazine ads and strolled past the local dealerships, memorizing the attributes of each auto and weighing the comparative values of price, mileage and pride of ownership. It wasn't long before we were driving out of the Bernard Brothers Cadillac dealership in Omaha behind the wheel of a 1954 Oldsmobile Super 88, a four-door sedan with Starfire hubcaps. We had indeed shattered the piggy bank and had plunked down $4,700 in cash to get that car. It was ours, and we were bursting with pride.

I'll never forget its bright red body and its shiny grill with the Olds logo of North and South America above it. The interior boasted rich wine-colored upholstery. It was long and sleek, but learning to parallel park it with those two protruding tail lights was a real challenge. "If I don't dream now, 'I can make it!' I won't even come close," I had once mused. I knew I was on the right path now.

Sitting in the driver's seat of that car fulfilled many of my fantasies, and, like a sixteen-year-old who has just passed his driving test, I was ready to go anywhere and at any time. Gasoline averaged about twenty-one cents per gallon, so we could fill up the tank for a reasonable price and, until we decided what to do with the rest of our lives, Duane and I were free to take off whenever we felt like it.

Now that there was no longer any family to keep her in Canada, Mom had moved to Omaha from Vancouver to be nearer to relatives who lived in the United States. Shortly after getting to Nebraska, she learned that Miriam and her husband Eric had returned from Japan and were going to Minneapolis, and she immediately wanted to visit them. She asked if we would drive her there, and we agreed with alacrity, excited at the prospect of trying out our new car on the open road. Many years would pass before the inauguration of the interstate highway system as we know it today, but it was still only about a 400 mile ride. As it turned out, that trip offered us another insight into "Mom's" character at the same time that it once again provoked more questions than answers.

When Dad had used the explanation of a nervous breakdown for our aunt's behavior, we had readily accepted his words because we had little understanding of either mental or physical illnesses. Almost nothing was written for laymen on psychiatric or psychological aberrations in the 1940s, and I'm not sure even Dad understood what went on in her head. We only knew what manifested itself in inconsistent behavior, vacillating as it did between her treatment of her daughters and us and the face the general public saw. We had been mystified at the changes we observed when we had gone back to Edmonton from boot camp, and amazed that the woman who had once screamed, "I'm not your mother" had started to sign her letters *Mom*. There had also been her unnerving act of contrition when Dad died, and now, the woman who had barely spoken to us when we drove from Edmonton to Nebraska just eight years previously, was proposing we drive together for at least eight hours. The woman was an enigma, and clearly we would never understand what motivated her actions.

From Minneapolis, we continued to St. Paul to see her cousin Effie Nelson, who was the widow of a prosperous steel mill owner. Effie lived in a magnificent house, and driving to her home we admired her neighborhood, which was far grander than any we had known before. It was now that Mom dropped a little nugget of truth she had hidden all those miserable years we had suffered under her roof.

"When your father died," she told us, "Effie and her husband wanted to adopt you. But Dad and I couldn't let them, because we wanted you boys."

"Wanted?" I had never heard such rubbish! It was hard to swallow that at the time, and it is harder still for me today. Perhaps she couldn't live with the idea that her beloved daughters would grow up on a clergyman's salary while we, the orphans, dined on food prepared by a cook at Effie's and slept in beds made up by a maid. Nothing she said now could ever erase the memory of the nightmarish cellar; the years of toil were too fresh in our minds. Perhaps we wouldn't challenge her lies because she was Dad's wife, but neither could we accept such protestations of family togetherness. Much as the realization pained me, I was beginning to admit to myself that Dad's commitment to us had been prompted more by a sense of duty than of love, and that understanding didn't jibe with Mom's new comment. However, our lifelong devotion to our church and biblical teaching had also left its mark on us, so Duane and I felt an obligation to care for her as long as she lived. But that arrangement in no way dictated that we could ever believe she had wanted us, and we could never truly love her. Nevertheless, we did see that she always had everything she needed until she died in 1997 and was buried next to Dad in Vancouver.

I soon moved to Omaha, partly because it never occurred to me to settle anywhere except where Duane would be, and partly because that's where Ruth and Ray lived and I felt the pull of family. I cherished the memory of the Christmas we had spent with them in Milwaukee when we were students at the academy, and I looked forward to strengthening these ties. Unfortunately, since their return to Nebraska, Ray's prospects, which had seemed promising at the time of their wedding, had diminished. I know the rent we paid him while we lived with them made it easier for Ruth to handle her household expenses, since our contribution more than made up for feeding two extra mouths.

Now that Duane and I owned our own wheels, I needed to find a job to keep them in working order on the road. I soon landed a position with Union Pacific as secretary to the general passenger traffic manager. I stayed with the company for three years, grateful that the typing and shorthand courses I had mastered in Wahoo gave me a marketable skill. I found I really liked the business world and the camaraderie of the office workers, and I would have been content to stay there longer had I not realized my eligibility for the GI Bill was running out. I enrolled at the University of Omaha in the fall of 1958.

That year was unremarkable except that in my economics class I sat next to Peter Fonda, son of Henry Fonda, the celebrated actor. That brought Duane and me to another secondhand brush with fame when Peter's sister, Jane, came to visit a friend. Peter arranged for a small party, found another girl for me, and we triple-dated at a movie, followed by a hamburger. It would be about ten years before Jane would star in *Cat Ballou* and a long time before Peter would become a well-known actor, but they were the children of a famous father and that made the occasion a memorable evening. Not bad, I think now, for a boy who carried water when there was no indoor plumbing and built snow caves to warm himself on the way to school.

In 1959, after college let out for the summer, I was fortunate to land a job in Omaha at Gate City Steel, manufacturer of boilers and standpipes, earning about $400 per month. It was then that I realized that though I might be a lifelong learner and would eventually be an avid reader, I really preferred to pursue my education outside the classroom. About that time, I started keeping a dictionary by my side whenever I began a book. I was still suffering from an abysmal lack of study habits, and it severely handicapped my ability to juggle assignments and write papers. In addition, although I enjoyed the casual acquaintance of my fellow students, I was beginning to feel a little too old for campus frivolity.

In that frame of mind, I avidly jumped at the chance that summer to move to Cody, Wyoming, where I was promised a job as secretary to the president of Husky Oil for the then-generous salary of $735 per month. Although I had already celebrated my twenty-eighth birthday, I was still incredibly naive about company politics and much too trusting—I didn't realize that until later. A more cynical person than I would have questioned why the company would be willing to offer me such a generous salary, and it didn't occur to me that it could be an incentive to lure employees to a less than inviting climate. I discovered all too soon after I reached Cody that my career prospects were even less promising.

Dressed in a brand-new suit, I waited in the anteroom of the personnel office to fill out the proper papers and set up a time to meet the company president. I was anxious to get over the preliminaries and ready to prove my mettle. There was another young man already seated there when I arrived, and keen to share my good fortune but not wanting to boast, I asked, "You here for a new job, too?" His response floored me as he smilingly confided, "Yes, I'm the new secretary to the president."

"Wait a minute," I thought to myself, "that's why I'm here." The guardian angel of prospective employees must have been hovering at my shoulder, urging me to keep silent, so I just nodded noncommittally and went back to perusing my magazine. In reality I felt totally confused and asked myself, "What's going on? Who is this guy? What do I do next?"

I didn't have long to wait, and I was soon ushered into the vice president's office. In short order, I learned that the other man would be the president's secretary and worse still, not only had my original job offer been rescinded, but the enormous salary was equally illusory. My monthly stipend had been reduced to $400, and I was being hired as the secretary in the asphalt sales department. I was chagrined at how I had been duped, but the disappointments I had endured in the past had prepared me to pick up the pieces and just forge ahead. But this time, I didn't last long and ended up working there for six months.

I could only describe my new boss as a plodder. He accomplished everything in his job description, no more and no less, and his satisfaction with the status quo was well known throughout the company. He disliked innovation and avoided any technological improvements as if he knew that machines might replace him someday. He liked the comfort of feeling safe with the perks of his seniority. I, by contrast, chafed at continually doing things as they had always been done, and I knew that others in the office agreed. It was particularly annoying to prepare each purchasing form anew for every order when, as I remarked to the purchasing agent, "anyone can see how easy it would be to preprint them!"

This conversation took place while the boss was out of the office on vacation, and with the purchasing agent's permission, I sent the forms to a branch office to be duplicated. My boss came back, took one look at what I had done and, to put it mildly, all hell broke loose. He jumped to the conclusion that I had gone behind his back to curry favor with senior management, and I soon realized that my best form of action would be to write a letter of resignation. Clearly, although my attempt at efficiency might have been appreciated by my fellow workers and anyone directly affected by the new format, I was too new to buck the standards of seniority at Husky Oil. In the end, the vice president who called me into his office not only rejected my letter of resignation, but with an angry flick of his wrists, tore it in half and threw it at me. "You're fired," he pronounced. I had moved almost 900 miles geographically, but hadn't advanced nearly as far professionally.

Being fired was demoralizing to my ego, but I felt buoyed by Duane's appearance in Cody when he came to help me pack up my belongings. I had read an article in a back issue of *Holiday Magazine* about the Rocky Mountains and, remembering how impressed I had been with the scenery in Banff, I decided to relocate to Colorado.

It was 1960, and I had just turned twenty-nine when I arrived in Denver in early April, once more job seeking and once more a stranger in a new city. I can't say exactly why I chose the Mile High City, as I knew it was nicknamed, except I knew that I liked its reputation. Denver was definitely the largest metropolis in the region. I had heard that the people were friendly, the attitude laid back, and that it still offered something of the frontier spirit one hundred years after the whisper of gold had lured prospectors west. But I wasn't expecting to do any gold mining or panning, and since I had about fifty dollars in my pocket and little or no savings, I started looking for work the next day.

I read the employment section of the *Rocky Mountain News* and went to more than twelve different places for interviews. I still didn't know enough about the job market or about selling myself, for that matter, so I didn't have a résumé or even a mental list of my attributes. As I trudged from personnel office to personnel office and ticked off the circled boxes in the classifieds, I heard the same dispiriting comments, "Sorry, the job's been filled," or "We're looking for someone with experience."

After job hunting for six weeks and not finding anything, I finally asked to speak with the pastor at the Lutheran church on Alameda Avenue which I had been attending regularly. He agreed to contact a man in the congregation who was the manager of Snelling & Snelling Employment Agency in Denver to ask if he could give me some assistance in finding a job. Shortly after I called on this man for an appointment, he sent me to Continental Airlines to interview with the vice president of the advertising department. I was offered a job that same day. I started work before the end of May.

Over the years, I had developed a strong work ethic, and it wasn't in my nature to offer less than one hundred percent of myself in any endeavor. I threw myself into the new job, worked hard, and rarely took a lunch break, so anxious was I to master the ropes. I didn't realize that although this might endear me to my bosses, it could be a real detriment to relationships with my office mates. Soon thereafter, the three girls in that department, who were seen more often in conversations at the water fountain than bent over their typewriters, became annoyed at my diligence. I was getting much too much work accomplished while they discussed the weekend just past and planned for the one upcoming.

"Hey, Ed, they don't expect you to work this hard," they would remonstrate, but I lacked the social repartee to sidetrack their annoyance. They soon resented me for showing them up, and began to complain to our boss that if I stayed, they would all quit. Faced with the prospect of losing the services of four somewhat experienced clerks as opposed to one zealous newcomer, the leery manager soon called me into his office and gave me two weeks notice.

It wasn't in my nature to leave a project unfinished, so I went to the office that Saturday morning to complete my filing and clean up my desk. As I was putting the last of the papers in order, I came across a piece of correspondence from Mountain Bell that was signed by Jack Guenther, national Yellow Pages representative. I wrote his name down, and on Monday, I put in a call to him. When he came to the phone, I said, "My name is Edwin Vikman; I'm with Continental Airlines."At first he must have thought I was calling about the airline's account, but when I asked, "What would be the chance of getting a job with Mountain Bell?" he responded positively. "You couldn't have called at a better time; right now they're hiring."

He arranged for me to take a physical at the company's medical department, and while I was there, I met another fellow who was also applying for a job as a Yellow Pages salesman. Our exchange was eerily reminiscent of my conversation with the applicant at Husky Oil, but we exchanged phone numbers. A couple of days later he called with the question, "How do you like working for the Telephone Company?" "I haven't heard anything yet," I answered. "Oh, you will; I just heard today," my new friend responded. Well, I waited a week and when I still hadn't heard anything, I went to the Yellow Pages office and asked to speak to the division manager. "We don't have anything right now, but we'll keep you in mind," he promised, as he came out of his office.

Thus began another round of fruitless applications and interviews. Each morning I perused the help wanted pages, circling anything that had possibilities, and presenting myself to prospective employers for their inspection. Keeping my hopes high was difficult, but fortunately I had retained my frugal ways (except for buying the Olds which I still owned) and I had enough money for necessities.

One morning, when the job openings seemed particularly sparse, I put my pride in my pocket and presented myself once again at the Yellow Pages office. The same manager came out and said, "Frankly, the job requires sales experience, and you have none." I left, feeling completely depressed, but I wasn't ready to give up. I kept looking for work, but I just couldn't find anything. Only a few days later, when I was near the Yellow Pages office again, I thought to myself, "They seemed to like me, and I'm going to try one more time." The secretary looked up at me and said "May I help you?" Wasn't she tired of seeing my face by then? I took a deep breath and said, "Yes, I would just like to thank Mr. McFarland for even considering me for the job." Mr. McFarland must have heard me because he came out of his office and, putting his hand on my shoulder, nudged me toward the door saying, "Good luck to you." Clearly, he had seen enough of me.

I stopped and said, "Sir, I'm only sorry I didn't have a chance to prove myself because if I wasn't in the top 10 percent of your sales organization in six months, I would voluntarily leave, knowing the job wasn't for me."

He looked surprised at that, but replied, "Excuse me for a moment," and disappeared back into his office. I waited patiently in the anteroom for twenty-two minutes before he came back with the invitation to come into his office and close the door. I thought he was going to chew me out, but instead he astonished me with the words, "If you're willing to go to work on that basis, I'll hire you." Those were the days when the phone company paid only seventy-five dollars a month. Any additional salary was totally based on commission from sales. I think he must have thought it was worth $450 to get rid of this bum.

I went to work for Mountain Bell as a Yellow Pages advertising representative on February 2, 1962, and I discovered that I was a born salesman. When my customers saw me coming through their door, they knew that no matter how difficult their day had been, they would soon be laughing. I used jokes and banter to soften people up, especially if they were reluctant to take an ad or accept an increase, and I kept a diverse repertoire of stories.

I soon found that the long days I had endured when I lived at Carlsons' had ably prepared me for the prolonged hours of a salesman who is determined to succeed. Each representative was assigned to a crew whose size depended on the local population—while there would be six in a city the size of Colorado Springs (population approximately 150,000 in 1960), there would be two in a smaller municipality like Casper, Wyoming (population approximately 50,000 in 1960). Accounts were divided into three classes—A, B, or C—but each salesman started out on an even playing field, since the phone numbers in the book were divided equally among them without regard to size or category. After that, the real competition began, and I excelled at the challenge.

I was only home on weekends for about seven months of the year, and I made about ten calls a day, working from 8:00 a.m. until I felt like stopping. Many times that meant being on the job well into the evening when I called on bars and other businesses that stayed open late. But I loved every minute of it because I loved the people I met, and I reveled in my independence and my newly discovered talent. I came to know the best restaurants for my dinners like the City Café in Colorado Springs that advertised home cooked meals, and whenever I was new to a town I scouted out the nearest grocery store to buy chocolate milk and doughnuts for lunch. I looked for a convenient coffee shop for breakfast on the way to my first call, and I knew the location of every diner east of the continental divide and which had the cheeriest waitresses and served the best breads. I had my favorite seats and sat on the same swivel stools at their shiny Formica counters in most of them. Although I didn't want to waste time eating—I couldn't earn money that way—I recognized the importance of staying in a motel with comfortable beds where I could be sure of getting a good night's rest, and I had my favorite lodging spots, too. Being tired and grumpy after tossing on a lumpy mattress was a surefire way to lose a sale.

When I started with Mountain Bell, we were given a per diem allowance of fifteen dollars, and I was able to save enough from that and my expense account to cover my monthly home mortgage of $158.84 and some house maintenance as well. So much has changed since the introduction of the Internet to popular communications that it is difficult to remember, today, how dependent people were on their ever available Yellow Pages directory. Whether a person needed a housepainter, or a doctor, or the name of a neighborhood restaurant, that was the first source of information that came to mind, and it usually provided the needed answer. The previous year's edition was usually dog-eared and ready for disposal when the newest one appeared on the doorstep. Being a successful salesman for such an important household item meant not only a steady income, but a sense of accomplishment as well.

Duane had been working for Northwestern Bell for three years in Des Moines, when he and his wife, Farrel, moved to Denver in 1968. Soon after, he joined me at Mountain Bell which was known for offering the best commissions and working conditions. How I enjoyed it when we were occasionally assigned to the same crew and could meet for lunch. In recent years, our lives had followed different patterns, but nothing could ever diminish the ties of our twinship, and we were equally content either trading sales tips and amusing anecdotes or sharing companionable silence.

One day, I noticed that the sweater our regular waitress at the City Café in Colorado Springs was wearing was fraying badly at the cuffs. When I mentioned it to Duane, he immediately responded, "Let's go buy her a new one when we're finished." I remembered that her old one was blue, and we replaced it with one that was almost the identical color. I still received the same rush of satisfaction from helping someone as I had when I bought dinners for the men in Beaver City. I liked assisting people who hadn't prospered as I had. Stopping for a newspaper one morning when we were working east of Pueblo in La Junta, Colorado, I saw that the newsboy rode a bicycle with only one pedal. When I spoke to him, he told me that he didn't have any money to repair it since he gave all his earnings to his mother every week. I found out where he lived and told his mother I would like her permission to buy him a new one (the memory of Duane and me sharing one dilapidated bicycle when we were at Carlsons' prompted this thought). The next morning I bought him a bright red Schwinn. His astonished cry of delight reverberates in my ear whenever I think of him. I hadn't forgotten Dad's admonition as he left us at Edna Nelson's in 1946 that the true measure of a man is how he treats someone who can do him absolutely no good.

"How I love this job," I frequently thought when I returned to the home office and viewed the big board on the wall that listed the names of the salespeople and their performance, including the increase and loss in their production. My name was always at the top, and I was rewarded with many trips as a result. I was never below the top ten percent in the company during my tenure. There were 187 people on the sales force in eight states. I won every award the company had to offer many times and was asked on several occasions to write articles for the company newspaper on the secret of my success. One time I joked, "It's the same stuff that makes grass grow green." They responded, "We can't print that," and my comment was often repeated, but never printed.

I retired on September 21, 1985, when the Bell System was broken up. I was always honest with my clients and looked out for them first, not giving any thought to my commissions. I had a wonderful career, and I thank God every day for the terrific job I had all those years.

I had dreamed I could make it. And I had.

Epilogue

My early life was harsh. I don't know how Duane and I survived. We didn't really start living until we were fifteen years old—everything else before that was a learning experience.

I don't know why I was never jealous of other boys, or why I never stole anything, and I don't remember telling any lies to make excuses. Somehow, throughout all that happened, I held on to the sense of personal dignity that is essential to human survival, and I became the man I am today. I took pride in everything I did. I know I was always inquisitive. From an early age there was nothing I wouldn't try to do—plumbing, electrical wiring, painting, farming, trucking, and building my model railroad.

I have always been there to help anyone who asked because I have never forgotten the misery I felt as a lonely and neglected little boy. I don't know what I would have done without my twin—I think Duane and I literally saved each other. We had one another and our faith in God.

What I missed growing up, however, was a role model to imitate and to learn from in developing and fostering successful personal relationships. I don't know if Dad and Mom were happy together, but I certainly never enjoyed a normal family life either with them or in any of the homes where Duane and I spent our childhood. Probably because of this, we never thought we would marry; we thought we would just take care of one another as we always had. We never considered that we might fall in love or, perhaps most significant, that someone else might find us lovable.

I guess it was a surprise to me, then, when one of the women that I was dating rather casually suggested we should get married. I suppose it was my desire for a home and family that caused me to agree. However, it proved to be a disastrous idea and our marriage was doomed from the start. Neither of us understood the importance of compromise and we hadn't been seeing each other long enough to realize how incompatible we were. Despite my material success, my wife and I were two desperately unhappy people. We lived in a beautiful home in a nice part of Denver and had two young children, but we never succeeded as a family. We had completely different desires and goals. In addition to this, my wife hated Colorado and missed her old home and parents. After just a few years she left and returned to Nebraska with our children. The divorce was devastating for all of us, and once again I was part of a broken and shattered family. I have never stopped loving my children who are always in my thoughts, and it breaks my heart that they have chosen to distance themselves from me.

My greatest consolation during that time was that Duane had also moved to Denver, and I knew he was always there for me. It reminded me of old times when we could be together.

I continued to prosper financially and enjoyed filling my home with beautiful furniture and artwork that I collected in my travels, but it was always empty when I returned. Strangely, with all the deprivation I had endured, I had rarely lived alone.

When I first moved to Denver, I joined the Augustana Lutheran Church. I attended regularly and became an usher at the Sunday services. One week at the coffee hour I met a particularly attractive young woman named Nancy. I knew that she had just joined because she was wearing the red carnation that was always given to new members. We chatted, but then didn't see one another for quite a while.

Taking up the collection one Sunday, I noticed Nancy again and saw she had filled out the registration form. I very surreptitiously took advantage of this opportunity to learn her phone number and shortly thereafter called her to invite her out on a date. Visiting married friends and observing families at church had taught me a great deal more about living with people. I now knew how I wanted to spend the rest of my life, and this time it was I who did the courting. I took Nancy to dinner at special restaurants, and we slowly became better acquainted. I gradually understood how much we loved one another and with eagerness I anticipated our future together.

How I enjoyed buying Nancy beautiful jewelry—and how I enjoyed the changes in my life. We went snowmobiling in Yellowstone National Park, explored the glories of the Rocky Mountains, and strolled through the narrow streets of old mining towns, all the time laughing and basking in each other's company. For the first time I knew the luxury of being totally at ease with someone besides my twin, and for the first time I experienced the freedom that comes with totally trusting another human being. Nancy and I became engaged on July 21, 1979, and we married that October. Together we have built a happy life.

If someone was to ask me now what is one of the most important messages I would like to share, I would tell them that Duane's and my story is not really one of misery and neglect, but rather an account of triumph over adversity. Despite the ugliness and neglect of our early life, and despite the fact that we were stripped of the most basic necessities and were subjected to the most deplorable living conditions, we overcame the cruelties of our childhood and youth. Instead of giving in to our misfortunes and permitting these hardships to shape our future, we steadfastly persevered and worked hard to gain what we wanted in our lives. As I said at the beginning of my story, I learned to see beyond the difficulties I encountered and to explore the deep wells of fortitude and faith that I found within myself. With the courage that produced, I could overlook the anger and meanness I met almost every day and found that I could both survive and succeed. That little boy who had depended on his twin brother's arms for both emotional and physical support, the little boy who had sought rainbows in puddles, had pierced the shadows of his cellar prison to discover the beauty and goodness of the world above and had become the man I am today. I want people to understand that it is not how a person is raised, but what they do with their lives, that's important. I simply want our story told.

Figure 1. The church in Timmervik, Sweden, from which the
Vikman name was derived in about 1920

Figure 2. Portrait of Edwin J. Vikman, father of Ed and Duane, the
day he graduated from the seminary in 1919

Figure 3. Hilma Carlson Vikman, mother of Ed and Duane, taken at an unknown date

Figure 4. J. Arvid (l.) and Edwin J. Vikman (r.) at Augustana College in Rock Island, Illinois, about 1919

Figure 5. Ed and Duane with their father in the parsonage garden in Genoa, Nebraska

Figure 6. Huldah Vikman, paternal aunt of Ed and Duane, circa 1920s

Figure 7. Aunt Huldah with Ed and Duane, before her return to Sweden

Figure 8. Older sisters Alice and Ruth with Ed and Duane, circa 1932

Figure 9. Ed and Duane in Genoa before their father died, 1932

Figure 10. Ed and "Dad" in Winnipeg, before the family moved
to Sweden, summer 1932

Figure 11. Ruth, Alice, Ed (l.), and Duane (r.) in Holdrege, Nebraska, when the twins returned from Sweden, 1935

Figure 12. Ed and Duane at Edna Nelson's farm in Nebraska, where they lived for a short while in 1937

Figure 13. The house in Edmonton, Alberta, where Ed and Duane
lived in the cellar (1940-1946)

Figure 14. Vikman family portrait—Linnea, Aunt Hildore, Miriam, and
Arvid "Dad", seated, with Ed and Duane on floor,
about the only time the twins were allowed in the living room

Figure 15. Ed and Duane, with the Carlson family dog, in the jackets they wore all winter regardless of the temperature (1943-1944)

Figure 16. A snow cave Ed and Duane built for protection from harsh winter weather on their four-mile walk to school in Camrose

Figure 17. The twins in their one-room schoolhouse in rural Camrose.
Ed is seated on the left, Duane at the other end of the row (1943-1944)

Figure 18. The washing machine at the Carlson farm

Figure 19. The cream separator the boys used to extract the cream after milking the cows each morning before school

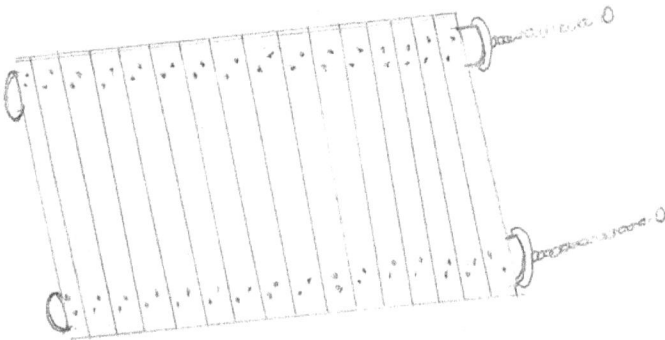

Figure 20. The stone boat, Ed and Duane's ingenious adaptation of a sled that they used to haul water for the family's washing and cooking

Figure 21. Ed and Duane with the team of horses, Jerry and Fly, that pulled the farm wagon in Camrose. The picture is dated April 29, 1943.

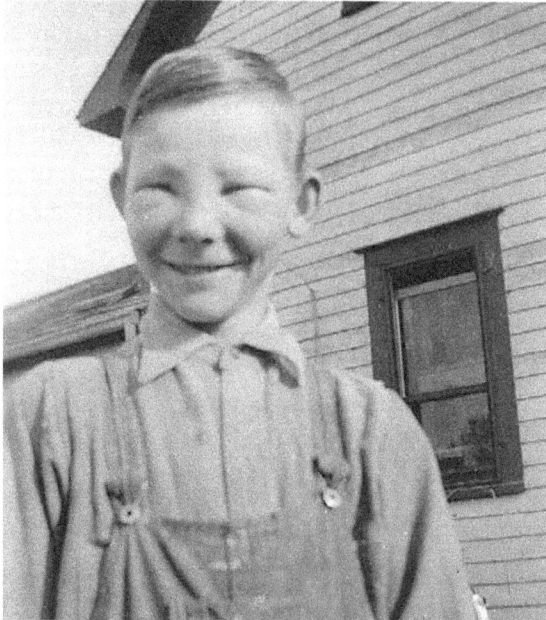

Figure 22. Duane, with a swollen face after stumbling into a hornets' nest while working at the Carlson farm, circa 1944

Figure 23. Ed and Duane with the Carlson family in front
of the farmhouse in Camrose, Alberta. Circa 1944

Figure 24. In Edmonton, Ed and Duane posed with their
confirmation class wearing their first suits, May 1945

Figure 25. The occasion of Ed and Duane's confirmation
even merited a formal portrait, May 1945

Figure 26. A long way from Wahoo, Nebraska, Ed and Duane
enjoyed their reunion in Hawaii during the Korean conflict, 1952

Figure 27. Duane (l.) and Ed (r.) pictured in the Edmonton newspaper, with an account of their service in Hawaii

Figure 28. Duane (l.) and Ed (r.) in Ed's garden in Denver, July 2005

Figure 29. Portrait of Nancy and Ed, taken for the church directory at
Augustana Lutheran Church, August 2005.
Photo by Lifetouch, Inc.

About the Author

Mary "Corky" Treacy Thompson embarked on her third career with the writing of this book. A stay-at-home mom and professional volunteer actively involved for many years in PTA, scouting, and the athletic and social activities of her daughter and two sons, she then followed a professional, paid path as the Alumnae Director of her Alma Mater, Manhattanville College and as the Executive Director of the Westchester Association of Insurance and Financial Professionals. During that time, she actively served in the social justice ministries of the Immaculate Heart of Mary Church in Scarsdale, New York, and in 1993 was elected to the first of two terms on the Board of Education where she was also the president in 1997–1998. In 2003, Corky and her husband Greg moved to Heritage Eagle Bend in Aurora, Colorado, where she continues her community involvement and is a member of the Society of St. Vincent de Paul at Our Lady of Loreto Catholic Church. She has been a mentor to incarcerated women in the Making Choices program at the Denver Women's Correctional Facility for eight years. In her leisure, Corky enjoys books, travel, and the time she and her husband spend with their family, which now includes seven grandchildren in Colorado, Virginia, and Connecticut. As a preteen, Corky aspired to be another Louisa May Alcott, holing up in her attic to write short stories on an orange crate, but laughs at the realization that it took her sixty plus years to complete her first book.

Laura Mahony Photography
Denver, CO